D1263918

The i·mpossible Project: Volume 2

Changing Minds, Breaking Stigma, Achieving the Impossible

Joshua Rivedal

Candace Rivedal

50 Authors

Foreword

Stephen L. Mandel, M.D.

Skookum Hill Publishing
BEVERLY HILLS, CALIFORNIA

2017

Skookum Hill Publishing
369 S. Doheny Dr. #197
Beverly Hills, CA 90211

Thematic Editor: Joshua Rivedal
Copyeditor: Pamela Cangioli
Cover Design: Sobola Damilare
Book Layout: Joshua Rivedal

Ordering Information:
Quantity sales. Special discounts are available on quantity purchases by corporations, associations, and others. For details, contact the "Special Sales Department" at the address above. Contact the author directly at http://www.iampossibleproject.com for special fund-raising opportunities for charitable organizations.

The i'Mpossible Project: Volume 2: Changing Minds, Breaking Stigma, Achieving the Impossible/ Joshua Rivedal, Candace Rivedal.
ISBN 978-0-9860964-1-9

Acknowledgments

We would like to thank our family for their love and support. We especially want to thank the people listed below. They were early adopters of this book and believed that a book on overcoming mental illness was truly "possible," and for that we are truly grateful. And to all of our authors in this book, you are incredible human beings—brave, talented, inspirational, and committed to preventing others from needless suffering due to mental illness or another personal difficulty. Thank you so much.

- Joshua & Candace

Rick Strait, Mary Jo Connell, Theresa Keown, Jensen McGinness, Phyllis Blackwelder, Roberta Bennett, Jamie Smith, Ellen Cole, Lee Moorhead, Blair Snyder, Angela Finley, Michelle Granahan, Alyson Kriewaldt, Sandra J. Williams, Laurie Arslani, Sylwia Truszkowski, Suzanne Smith, Madison Schutze, Alyx Korn, Taylor Pearcy, Elizabeth Zapata, Kristen Skopek, Mike Roberto, Lara Brown, Ann Harman, Rachel Bates, Alison Montrim, Claude Matranga, Jodi Engebos, Lauren Wassner, Krista Parkinson, Tracy McLaughlin, Josie Baker, Troy Hanson, Kirsten Holsomback, Nichole Carstens, Mary Oldenburg, Michael J. Korpi, Kathleen Myre, Mellisa Nielsen, Michelle Mariscal, Clarissa Jacobsen.

Table of Contents

i'
Flipping the Script on "Impossible"

FOR AS LONG AS I CAN REMEMBER, I've been living with a nagging health condition—something that until age twenty-seven (only six years ago) I didn't even have words to describe.

As a kid, I would often go through bouts of extreme sadness for seemingly no reason at all. Sometimes my sadness would interfere with school work, friendships, and my self-esteem. As a teen, I figured out how to tolerate it but never learned how to manage it. As an adult, I went through the same bouts of extreme sadness but they began to ramp up to several times a year. At age twenty-seven, one bout of sadness left me suicidal and searching for answers. While recovering, I got into therapy, did loads of research, and found out what was causing my sadness: depression.

Just before age twenty-eight, I began to learn to manage my depression, and then started speaking openly all over the world about it because I didn't want one more person to experience the pain and suffering I once had.

While on my travels, I met thousands of people who had their own stories of hope, healing, and overcoming life's obstacles. Many of these people wanted to tell their story to help others, much like I was doing. This is where the first edition of The i'Mpossible Project was born. *Reengaging with Life, Creating a New You* was the subtitle and it featured authors with mental health conditions, trauma, suicide loss, and disabilities. January, 2016 the book was published and started strong out of the gate—and readers were asking for a second edition.

So, we listened. This second volume is all on people living with mental health conditions, how they've found ways to manage, and what they do to live a happy, healthy, and fulfilling life. These are seemingly ordinary people who have accomplished extraordinary feats in their lives—making the impossible, possible, and changing the world.

Why mental health? After working for more than five years in the field, and while managing my own ongoing depression, I realized—we as a society don't speak openly enough about mental health. We talk sports, dieting, sex, work, and how gluten-free muffins are better than the regular kind—but we don't talk nearly enough about how to keep our brains healthy. And I'm not just talking about someone being depressed, bipolar disorder, anxiety, or any other "disorder." I'm talking the good parts too: therapy, yoga, taking time off from work to rest, or binge-watching the Bachelorette (My wife got me hooked on this show. #facepalm). So... what's up with the book's subtitle?

CHANGING MINDS

This is one of my life missions, what we're working toward with our comprehensive training series on mental health, and what we're hoping to achieve with this book—to change people's hearts and minds when it comes to mental health and mental illness. But we're not going to force it. We're going to let you come to that conclusion yourself—after all, you are pretty darn smart… at least smart enough to buy this book (my editor wouldn't let me insert a winking emoji here. Buzzkill).

Breaking Stigma

If I could have written "Beating the $%^ Out of Stigma," instead of "Breaking Stigma" I would have—but I was advised against it. Stigma is a killer and prevents people from speaking up and getting help for something that: is treatable, is often a part of everyday life, doesn't make you less of a person but, in reality, more human. I detest stigma (also known in some cases as "prejudice," and "discrimination"). This book and these stories are part of the daily battle being waged against stigma surrounding mental health.

Achieving the Impossible

This is what The i'Mpossible Project is all about. Impossible is nothing more than a mindset. Of course, I'll never sprout wings no matter how badly I want to fly. But one thing I can do is find the essence of why I want to fly and find alternative ways to achieve it: become a pilot, take hang-gliding lessons, work on inventing a jetpack, become a flight attendant—and the list could go on. The aim of this book and the i'Mpossible series is to show people who are working toward what many believe is impossible and yet who are achieving it anyway.

For much of recent history, mental health was viewed by society as a conversation about "crazy." And people living with mental health conditions were viewed as pariahs—and living a healthy, productive, and fulfilled life was deemed impossible.

But as someone living with depression and who manages it through counseling, a support system, a pill, faith, creativity, and healthy habits—I'm living a healthy, productive, and fulfilled life, and I'm flipping the metaphorical bird at archaic societal views. And so are the authors in this book.

How This Book is Supposed to Be Read

Any way you want. You're the boss. Read it in order. Read it out of order. Read it to a friend. Or pass it to along to someone you care about. Some of the stories might be a difficult read, while others you'll breeze through. Take your time.

Each story is a thousand words—unique, powerful, and straight to the point. All are written with love and the hope that you will take something away that will help you through your day, your week, or the rest of your life.

This book is not written entirely by polished authors. But I've lightly edited each of the stories; not to fit my #snarky writing style, but rather to make sure the crux of each story is unmistakably clear.

And if you're anything like me, you've probably skimmed the last two pages thinking, "When is this guy gonna get to the point? When are we gonna get to the stories?" Hold on fellow skim-reader. We're almost there.

Ladies, gentlemen (or whatever gender you identify as #equality); I present to you: fifty authors, and fifty inspirational, life-changing stories.

i

....

Foreword
Stephen L. Mandel, M.D.

FIRST MET JOSH when my team and I were reaching out to suicide prevention organizations in the area. I came across the Matthew Silverman Memorial Foundation (MSMF), which really stood out to me as a wonderful organization dedicated to preventing suicide. Josh's wife Candace is the executive director of MSMF, and after reaching out and meeting with her, I became acquainted with Josh. Soon enough, Josh told me of a loved one, a prospective patient, who he felt would benefit from our IV Ketamine Infusion Therapy and connected us. That patient ended up coming in for treatment.

Josh and I began to talk more often. We began to collaborate towards our common goal—to prevent suicide. It was during that time that I was introduced to this book.

I read and enjoyed Josh's first book in the i'Mpossible book series very much. When Josh approached me to write the foreword for his second book in the series, *Changing Minds, Breaking Stigma, Achieving the Impossible,* I was thrilled to say, "Yes!"

Josh is an extraordinary person who had an amazing transformation from the depths of his depression seven years ago. He has devoted his life to shedding light on the possibilities for change for fellow sufferers. He is an inspiration for those of us who believe in paying it forward. The i'Mpossible Project, represents another step forward in his ongoing contribution to bring awareness to this cause.

This inspiring book resonates with me. The idea of paying it forward is what motivated me to leave my anesthesia practice and start Ketamine Clinics of Los Angeles three years ago, despite it being considered experimental and even reckless by many other practitioners. I felt there was enough research and enough suffering and loss to warrant the use of this important treatment. Depression and suicide are too prevalent, and the signs are often ignored. Suicide and depression is something I have faced in both my professional and family life.

Mental illness is not an easy journey. Major depressive disorder is the most common cause of disability in the United States—affecting approximately 14.8 million American adults, or about 6.7 percent of the U.S. population age 18 and older, in a given year *(Archives of General Psychiatry, 2005 Jun; 62(6): 617-27)].* Many of the authors of this book suffered from, and fought their way up from depression. This book explores a number of other mental illnesses as well, from schizophrenia, depression, anxiety, OCD, and suicidality to name a few.

When ketamine infusions were discovered to quickly and safely lift depression and reverse suicidality, I embraced the opportunity to make a difference for people in this way. It was a natural fit for me because of the master's degree I earned in clinical psychology before becoming an anesthesiologist; giving me the interest and a good foundation of knowledge in mental health. As an anesthesiologist, I have used ketamine extensively for over thirty-five years.

At Ketamine Clinics of Los Angeles, we are committed to providing treatment for those seeking relief from mental illness. We administer IV Ketamine Infusions to depressed and suicidal patients, as well as those suffering from other mood disorders and chronic pain. All of our patients are deemed treatment-resistant prior to arriving at my clinic. We understand that many of them are suicidal and have an urgent need for relief. IV Ketamine Infusions can dramatically and rapidly jump-start wellness and break people free from their depression and suicidality.

Ketamine infusions work quickly, often within a few hours or days. They are very effective; over 83% of our depressed patients get relief. Success is even greater for suicidal patients. I know that many of the people who are featured in this book would likely have benefited from ketamine infusions.

As I read this book, it immediately became a page-turner for me. The entries are short, poignant, heart-felt; raw and authentic. You can feel the courage of these authors who are paying it forward by contributing the details of their suffering and their transformation. Each story is unique and incredibly personal, with such detail it will make your heart crave more. There is a universal theme in all of them—how paying it forward, in acts of courage such as sharing these stories, can contribute to both their own therapeutic process as well as the well-being of others.

I witness many of our patients who benefit from ketamine also sharing their stories in this way. They become champions of the use of ketamine as a tool for the advancement of wellness. It is fascinating to see this transformation and rewarding to know that these people are now living well and functioning in ways they didn't think possible.

All those suffering wish to break free from the chains of their past. To all fifty authors in this edition of The i'Mpossible Project, I admire you for demonstrating your bravery in pursuit of relief that often seems elusive or impossible to attain at the time.

I acknowledge the writers and Josh too, for contributing to the richness of all of our journeys. Read this book and you will come away humbled, hopeful, and better equipped to deal with your own life challenges. Wishing you and yours, long-term health and happiness.

- Steven L. Mandel, M.D.

Founder, President
Ketamine Clinics of Los Angeles

....

Anxiety

"*TELLING SOMEONE WITH ANXIETY to just calm down is like telling someone with epilepsy to stop having a seizure.*"
 – Anon

Escaping Darkness, Choosing Light

Shannon Ackerman

TWO YEARS AGO, if you would have told me I would be alive today and helping change the world, I would have told you that you were crazy. Two years ago, I couldn't even see myself living to be sixteen, let alone making it to my sophomore year of high school.

At fourteen, I was moving schools and had issues with my paternal father. And I was being bullied at school, which started in elementary school and never really stopped. But it was middle school that had the biggest impact on me. I moved between three schools in three years, the last one being in Florida. The second one I attended in Colorado took the largest toll on me.

People made fun of me, a lot. I was taunted for being poor, overweight and for not being pretty enough. I had a face full of acne, I would shake a lot, and I had a hard time talking to people.

I could count the few friends I had on one hand, but there was constant drama. But none of this is what tore me apart.

A few days into March, my mom had picked me up from a cheerleading tryout. In the car, the words spilled from her lips, "Shannon, Uncle John V. committed suicide the other day..." She continued on but I couldn't hear a word she said. I felt like the floor had opened up from under my feet, swallowing me whole. My stomach dropped and I could feel my brain pounding against my skull. Tears welled up in my eyes as we pulled into the driveway of our house. I grabbed my backpack and headed downstairs into my room where I spent the rest of my night.

My uncle John V. wasn't a blood relative but I had known him since I was born. We'd watch football together and bond over our dislike of the Dallas Cowboys. He was sarcastic towards me, but was sweet to me and I looked up to him. The week he died was the first time I had grabbed a blade and dragged it across my wrist.

My life took a turn. I became isolated from my parents and I'd constantly get into arguments with my mom. I spent the majority of my time in my room and I stopped eating. I would not come out of the house and the only people I surrounded myself with were those who were a toxic part of my life.

The toxic people, I would somehow call "friends" kept telling me that I should "cut a little deeper" or "it should have been you instead" and for a while, I wished it were. I wanted to be dead.

We moved to Florida around eighth grade and I met some amazing friends, some of my best friends to this day, but even then, I still had an eating disorder and I was still self-harming.

And finally, I got tired of people seeing them so I took a blade to my thighs, which left countless of scars.

Though my friends tried to help, they had a hard time understanding and this carried on into my freshmen year of high school in Kentucky.

January 31st, 2015, I decided to recover and talk to my parents. I soon started going to my doctor and they recommended seeing a therapist. My therapist impacted my life so much, and we learned about two things that were controlling my life: anxiety and depression.

Throughout my newfound recovery, different medications have messed me up a bit and I have had a few relapses but I am better than I have ever been. And I owe that to my parents, my teachers, my friends, and my family.

Now, as a senior in high school, I am an active volunteer with the Matthew Silverman Memorial Foundation and have created a close bond with the foundation's executive director who will never know how much she has impacted my life. I received the foundation's Matt's Hero Award, which I will forever cherish.

The greatest thing I have learned throughout my journey is that I will be okay... and so will you. I cannot promise happiness, but I can promise that you will be okay. You have a choice, you can let people put a label on you and become that, or you can use your words, and you can move toward something greater than you can ever imagine.

There is good in the world, and good people, and the world is more kind than what it's made out to be.

We have a choice to be the light in the world, or we can stay hidden in the darkness. Tragedies can occur everywhere, even in our own lives. But please do not give up on the world, on other people, and especially not yourself.

i'

....

Chasing Butterflies
Nate Crawford

STAND HERE, THE END OF MAY in the yard of my rented farm-house. My three sons are standing around me. They are young and have the whole world in front of them, all of the awe that children have. They are six, two, and one, wide-eyed and curious, taking in life the way it should be. And, of course, they notice the butterflies. There are three of them flying in the air. And we run and we chase them. We chase these former insects now in their full beauty, trying to capture them, but not really because that would take away from the fun, from their beauty. So, we chase.

And as we chase, I forget where I am—fully engrossed in the moment. I am one more young child simply trying to touch the untouchable. The butterflies get away and we laugh and fall in the grass and simply enjoy the moment.

As I sit in this moment, I look up and see the window to my bedroom, the one I share with my wife. That room was the scene of a much different moment just a year earlier.

* * *

"I can't live like this. I can't live with you," my wife said, barely able to look at me.

I was crushed, destroyed. I looked at her and knew she was serious. She had never threatened divorce before. She had always said that we would make it, but I had finally become too much. My depression was destroying not only me, but her as well. She was afraid it would take my kids down too.

I have battled depression for my entire life. I had my first anxiety attack when I was seven. I have always had thoughts that the world would be better off without me, but when I was eleven, I started to indulge in suicidal ideation, meaning that my thoughts became more pointed and vivid. I had thought of how I might harm myself, how I might end my life. As a teenager, I thought this was normal—I mean, we always hear about how moody and weird teens are. They are not supposed to have these thoughts, though. No one is. But, the counselor that my parents sent me to saw me as everyone else did...a good student, a good kid, not a problem, maybe a little moody. I was told to go and that I did not need counseling.

When I reached college, I began to have sleepless nights caused not by study or partying, but because I was so fidgety and my mind moved so fast. My suicidal thoughts became more and more vivid to the point that I did not know if I could control the urges. I finally went to a counselor who immediately sent me to get meds. I was misdiagnosed as having a depressive episode. My anti-depressants caused my mind to race so fast, that I could not keep my legs still, and my hands twitched constantly. I could not live like this and yet I could not stop taking my meds. I was not depressed anymore, anyway.

For the next several years, I battled my demons but kept them hidden. I fell in love, got married, finished a master's degree and was in the middle of finishing my doctorate when my depression began to overtake me again. I went to my doctor who prescribed another anti-depressant. It did nothing. He upped my dosage. I still felt nothing but pain. He upped my dosage once more. My pain, hurt, suffering increased. I was dying inside and doing so quickly. My wife saw it. My doctor upped my dosage again.

Finally, we came to the point where she told me that she could no longer live with me. She might love me, but living with me had become so unbearable that our love could not sustain it. She issued me the ultimatum: "Get help or I'm leaving." I told her that I was simply doomed to my depression, but I called a counselor and saw him the next week.

When I saw the counselor and began to talk, he stopped me and asked if I had ever seen a psychiatrist.

"No, no one has ever said I needed to," I told him.

"Having the experience of an anti-depressant not working on you should have caused your doctors to send you to a psychiatrist rather quickly," he replied. He also went on to tell me that I was not simply in the midst of a depressive episode ("episodes" do not last years). I had something else and I needed to be seen by a psychiatrist. I called my doctor immediately and after a fight, he agreed to send me to a psychiatrist.

After two sessions with my psychiatrist, she diagnosed me with bipolar II disorder with an anxiety disorder on top of that. I was depressed, but also anxious and my depression came with hypomanic episodes. It felt good to have a name for what I was going through, to have something to fight, to deal with. I knew I would never get rid of my bipolar II, but I would continue to fight.

* * *

Ten months later, I sit in that yard, with my three sons, and enjoy the moment. I am not cured, am not ok. I still have much to deal with in my life and with my diagnosis. However, I am on the track to getting better, to recovery, to managing my symptoms. I know that my life will not be perfect but moments like this, times when I chase butterflies, make it all the more important to fight for my life.

My wife walks out and yells, "Lunch, boys." We get up and run inside, fueling to chase butterflies another day.

i

....

Breaking Free
Reece Anderson

I WAS TWENTY-YEARS-OLD and returning home from another intense tennis training. As I sat down to rest my legs, an unbearable surge of anxiety flowed through my body like a million electric shocks all at once. It felt like I was in a sprint race but standing completely still. My heart had elevated to an unhealthy 160 beats per minute—my first panic attack.

Young, naïve and in desperate need for a "cure," I started taking a daily antidepressant prescribed by our family doctor the day after my first panic attack. I felt a sense of relief that this pill—which I knew nothing about—could cure me. But soon my life turned into something chronic as one daily pill became two, then three, and then four.

My panic and anxiety suddenly formed TICS (Involuntary Movements). These movements would get so bad that when I was watching television my head would shake from side to side, I would click my shoulder on my left side over a thousand times a day, and consistently rub my forehead like an eraser. I formed habits to try and disguise my TICS. I would always wear a cap or sunglasses on my head so that my TICS could be mistaken for a quick adjustment of their position.

I began taking Xanax just to get me through the workday, which left me feeling drained and depressed afterward. I was also extremely self-conscious of my TICS to the point that I would avoid social situations with people I hadn't met before or large crowds. My anxiety and TICS lead to depression and at its worst I felt I could no longer live and seriously contemplated suicide.

For years, I was searching for something or someone to help me out of this black hole. I blamed the world and so many other things, until one day I looked at myself in the mirror. I realized that the person staring back at me was the only one who could stand up and start to find the real Reece under all the numbness and constant anxiety. I had let my anxiety and my TICS, consume me, own me, and prevent me from being the best version of me.

It was time to take back my life and own my actions. I wanted to be medication free, yet all my doctors were telling me this was not possible—the pills were a life sentence. But I had lost faith in the health system, as the pills I was prescribed did nothing except numb me and worsened my symptoms.

In March 2013, after returning home from seeing a good friend marry his soul mate, it clicked that I was never going to meet my own "Mrs. Right," till I started truly owning my situation. The day I arrived home I vowed to quit one pill immediately, cold turkey, no more. I had no strategy, no plan—I just stopped it.

My body showed very few after effects, and one year later I stopped number two but this time with a plan and the right support as I knew my body would give way at some point. Soon enough, my body started to fight back at me, telling me horror stories, as my TICS began to flare up again. But nothing could prepare me for coming off the third and final pill—the original medication I was given at age twenty. No amount of preparation could have helped me with what hit me next. Fourteen years of emotional numbness punched me square in the gut. I felt like I was back at the scene of that first panic attack every day for months on end. Everything I tried to do became increasingly difficult. The thought of going back on the pills haunted me daily—but I was out to find true me and I had to put up the fight of a lifetime.

Now eighteen months free of any medication, I've grown from not feeling anything to a man feeling like he can conquer the world. I can now appreciate the small things in life. And, of course, I could spend my days consumed by anger that those pills took nearly fifteen years of my life away—but, in fact, they made me the person I am today. I now have self-confidence, an awareness of my body and my health, and it has made me appreciate myself as a human being. Most of all, I met the love of my life in my partner Vicky, my stepdaughter Belle, and our new addition, eight-month-old Eden. Because I found myself through the long and winding journey overcoming TICS and prescription pills, life opened up doors and gave access to people I never thought were possible to have.

But most of all I know who I am and what I stand for—I found the real Reece.

i'

....

Reconnecting with Myself and My Life Worth Living

Tanya J. Peterson, NCC

KNEW I WAS LIVING A LIFE worth living. I *knew* it; I did not, however, always *feel* it. The knowledge that I loved my life and the people in it was there somewhere in some obscure part of my brain. That brain took the intellectual knowledge that I had created happiness and locked that knowledge into a fold, and with it, what felt like the essence of me.

Our family has a pet tortoise. She's a cute little thing that likes to get out of her box so she can tuck herself away and hide in a nook or a cranny. From the safety of said cranny, she observes. That was me, tucked tortoise-like inside a hard shell inside a brain fold. Observing. Alive and present, but not fully experiencing the way I was accustomed to doing.

While the essence of me was a tortoise in a fold, the brain surrounding me was electrified, buzzing with uncomfortable, unrelenting intensity. My brain seemed to have a life of its own, and I was at its mercy. I retreated into that fold on April 13, 2004, and remained in that watchful state for too many years.

On that fateful April 13, I was driving with my young children when we were struck from the side in an uncontrolled intersection, causing us to spin and roll fully over. Always one to focus on the positive, I did so even then: neither of my kids was injured, and all three of us were alive.

Focusing on the positive, on what is truly right and well, isn't Pollyanna fluff. It's perspective and choosing one's focus. Research in numerous psychological disciplines (positive psychology, acceptance and commitment therapy, cognitive-behavioral therapy (CBT), dialectical behavior therapy (DBT), and more) has shown time and again that the perspective we take and the thoughts we choose to accept or let go has a profound impact on our mental health and well-being. From the depths of personal experience, I can confidently attest to the power of perspective.

After the initial head injury, I sustained two more concussions in separate incidents. Some additional life stresses added to the brain injuries, and it all combined into a swirling, viscous mess. However, I was still the observing tortoise in that fold, and I kept my perspective to shape my values and actions.

True, I was only experiencing the positive on an intellectual level. I definitely wasn't functioning well enough to embrace life the way I wanted to. From the fold, I saw myself living life, and there was a lot of good despite the downs. Frustratingly, the real me was stuck in that tortoise shell, unable to fully feel the good but absolutely able to feel the struggles.

Concentration became an issue, as did memory and any ability to problem-solve (spending more than an hour trying to figure out how to strap a simple booster-seat to a chair was a signal that something was clearly wrong with my brain). My moods were all over the place, high and low multiple times a day. Random things made me irritable, something that was new to me. I became impulsive, especially with spending. And overarching all was unrelenting anxiety. I worried about past, present, and future. I felt guilty and full of self-blame. Constantly I feared the judgment and opinions of others. Something was wrong, and I didn't like it.

To get back on track, I began therapy. I came closer to being able to fully experiencing the good in my life again. However, I wasn't able to deal with the anxiety and mood problems. Driven by the knowledge that my life was good and I wanted to get back to living it fully, I voluntarily checked myself into a behavioral health hospital ninety miles from the town where I lived.

Admittedly, doing so initially increased my anxiety. What would people say? How would they treat my kids? What if it didn't work? What if I didn't like what they had to say?

That last fear came true. I didn't enjoy the diagnoses of bipolar 1 disorder, generalized anxiety disorder, and social anxiety disorder. I didn't like it when it took a long time discover the right combination of medication and therapy. I didn't like it when the antianxiety medication made my anxiety increasingly worse. I didn't like having to return to the hospital four more times over the course of a few years.

I didn't like a lot of things, but there was a lot more I did like. I liked being able to fully focus on the positive. I liked being able to not just know my passion and purpose but once again take an active role in choosing my attitude and behaviors in order to achieve them. I liked being able to fully experience my full life rather than just witnessing it on an intellectual level. I loved emerging from the fold, shedding the shell, and living my life worth living.

As Isaac Bittman tells his doctor in my novel *Twenty-Four Shadows*, "I'm here to get better so I can live a happy, normal life."

i

....

Where Deep Gladness Meets the World's Needs

Kendal Kooreny

EVERY MORNING, AS I WAKE and my eyelids open, I face the same, monotonous, unending pain. Every one of my joints is saturated with hurt. My energy is nowhere to be found. Headaches pound endlessly in my skull. Who knew a miniature, Lyme disease-infested tick could instigate such radical transformation in my health? Who knew a tick bite could result in my consumption of eighty pills per day (no, that's not an exaggeration), a port in my arm, and weekly intravenous infusions? Who knew a miniscule creature could create such overwhelming pain in my joints, my head, my stomach, and my entire body?

I will never forget the day I was diagnosed with Lyme disease in 2014—I was only fourteen years old. For years, countless doctors dismissed my symptoms as "growing pains" or a "desperate desire for attention," discounting the very real pain I experience constantly. When I first learned my blood tested positive for Lyme, I didn't know how to feel; I was excited to abandon the uncertainty and desperation that accompanied years of searching for a diagnosis, yet I was also devastated and terrified because Lyme is a serious illness with no definite cure.

Little did I know this single event would result in newfound purpose and trajectory for my life as well as awaken the fighter within me.

To put it lightly, battling a chronic, debilitating disease isn't easy physically or mentally. It has robbed me of things I previously took for granted: the ability to function like a normal teenager, spending time with friends when I now spend countless hours in bed, and playing golf on the high school team. It also created for me an abundance of daily anxiety, depression, and frustration. But I wouldn't change this tremendously difficult experience because of what my health battle developed within me—strength, perseverance, and compassion.

You couldn't guess by glancing at me that I am sick or that I follow an extensive treatment regimen. On the outside I resemble a normal, healthy teenager, which often causes people to doubt that I struggle with this invisible, chronic, nasty disease every second of every day. It can be discouraging when people refuse to believe I'm sick just because I seem okay on the outside, but if there's one thing I've learned through this process, it's that eve-

ryone fights some sort of metaphorical battle—health or other-
wise, visible or not—and everyone deals with some struggle at one
point or another.

I never imagined viewing anything Lyme disease-related as
less than a nightmare, especially my plethora of anxiety-inducing
food intolerances, but now I view it all as a blessing. My food intolerances forced me to focus meticulously on my nutrition. I vo-
raciously studied anything and everything I could find about food
and the science behind it. The more I read, the more I became
intrigued.

I also realized although we might have a plan for our lives,
nothing is ever certain, but that's okay. By being flexible and embracing uncertainty, you'll better be able to focus on the positive
aspects of any daunting situation.

Before my diagnosis, I thought I figured out the perfect plan
for my life: I would play varsity golf and take a full schedule of
advanced classes all throughout high school. I am a nerd with an
insatiable appetite for learning—not to mention a mean golf
swing. Eventually I would study in college to become a lawyer or
a fashion magazine editor. But I could never have imagined that
my disabling joint pain would force me to lay my clubs down and
that the Lyme disease would cloud my thoughts, preventing me
from understanding anything I read.

In spite of it all, I discovered a glimmer of silver lining—
throughout my studies into food and science, I developed a passion for health and nutrition that I couldn't wait to share with
others. This is how my blog *Health and High Heels* launched.
Health and High Heels began as a small Instagram account but
now has expanded across multiple social media platforms, which

I currently run to inspire and educate others about healthy living. I also cater charity events and speak to large audiences about my story. I learned to use my pain in a way that brings both myself and others joy in the process.

Author Frederick Buechner describes purpose as "the place where your deep gladness meets the world's needs." This quote resonates with me because the world possesses few Lyme disease and nutrition pioneers. I now know I will study nutritional science in college then proceed to medical school to become a doctor and help others like me, counseling people on ways food can heal the body.

Even though my war versus Lyme disease has been the most arduous adventure of my life both physically and mentally, it has also been the most fruitful. Without it, I would never have founded *Health and High Heels*, and I would still be on my way to studying something in college that was not intended as my destiny. I learned to find joy despite difficult circumstances, to discover purpose amidst pain, to readjust my expectations, to live with thankfulness rather than disappointment, and to persevere in the midst of hardship. I remind myself of these lessons whenever the trap of self-pity engulfs me, and even though sometimes doing so is immensely difficult, I wake up every morning with a smile because I believe that one miraculous day I will feel better, and hey, maybe today will be that day!

ADHD

"MY THOUGHTS ARE LIKE butterflies. They are beautiful, but they fly away."

- Anon

Turning the Whole Thing on its Head

Penny Williams

WHEN MY SON WAS DIAGNOSED with ADHD in 2008, it felt like my world came crashing down on top of me. No parent wants to hear that their child has a disability. I certainly didn't. There are parents who will tell you that they wouldn't change their child's disability, but they're kidding themselves. Of course we don't want to see our kids struggle and agonize.

Nonetheless, ADHD was the hand our family was dealt. It turned out to be a lot more than that: autism, anxiety, and dysgraphia were added to my son's alphabet soup of diagnoses in the years since.

I spent the first two or three years desperately seeking a "fix" for my son. I read dozens of books. I searched the internet for hours every day. I stalked online forums and discussion groups. I spent the majority of my days, for years, looking for an answer that didn't exist. In seeking to "fix" it, I was asking all the wrong questions and spinning my wheels in the muck that is developmental disorders. I had undertaken a self-assigned mission that could never be completed—because there is no cure, no "fix" for ADHD, autism, and learning disabilities.

When I finally realized that I was approaching my son's disabilities all wrong, I was a little surprised. I couldn't believe that not one doctor or therapist had steered me in a better direction. Frankly, I was appalled. How could they hand us a diagnosis and a prescription, and not teach us the fundamentals of *successfully* parenting kids with ADHD? *How?*

I immediately began asking better questions and setting more appropriate goals—how can I help my son develop coping strategies? learn lagging skills? Achieve success? As soon as I shifted my perspective and my goals for my son and my parenting, our struggles started improving and our entire family let out a collective sigh of relief. The realization that we *could* improve things—that life still could be rewarding and joyful—was monumental. That positive shift was incredibly empowering.

Room for retrospection opened up as life with ADHD, autism, anxiety, and dysgraphia settled just a bit. I could see that there was a better way to approach my son's disabilities the moment I stopped striving to "fix" it. I was angry that my family had to suffer longer than necessary. I was angry that there are millions of families and kids enduring intense struggles every day. I was angry that our kids were so often written off and left to fall through the cracks.

That's when I decided to turn this special brand of parenthood on its head—by helping other parents on a similar journey to struggle a lot less than we had.

I started by writing books on parenting kids with ADHD. I shared my personal family stories with the world, to show others they're not alone with these parenting struggles. I compiled what I found to work for families of kids with ADHD into a step-by-step guidebook for successfully parenting kids with ADHD. I even surveyed and interviewed nearly 100 adults who grew up with ADHD to know what the experience is like, and to learn what individuals with ADHD *really need* growing up. I still had an insatiable thirst for ADHD knowledge and insight, but now I was properly channeling it; I was turning it into a positive, by sharing to help others.

The more I shared, the more my passion for helping families raising challenging kids and challenging learners grew. I recently expanded my outreach to include online training courses and coaching, so I could take a more active role in personally guiding these special families to improvement.

I've always had an interest in public-spirited endeavors and helping others—I just didn't know it would be guiding and mentoring families raising kids with ADHD and autism to struggle less and triumph more.

Not only am I able to help others, but it's so fulfilling and nurturing for me as well. It gives my life a gratifying purpose, something I'd been seeking for quite a long time. The curse of ADHD and autism turned out to be a true blessing in my life. Would I make my son neurotypical if I could? Absolutely! In a heartbeat.

Since that's not possible, I just make lemonade instead, and it's delightful.

i'

....

Having a Child with ADHD has Made me a Better Person

Cristina Margolis

T'S NO SECRET THAT PARENTING is hard work. When you have a child with ADHD (Attention Deficit Hyperactivity Disorder), parenting can be much more difficult and complicated. It's been almost two years since we found out my seven-year-old has ADHD. Every day is a rollercoaster for us filled with ups and downs. When my child wakes up in the morning, I never know if she will be excited to go to school and see her best friend or have an epic meltdown and cry that she hates school. When it is time to get ready for bed, I never know if she will happily get into her pajamas and be excited about the story I'm going to read to her or cry and complain that she didn't have enough time to play that day. My child is extremely unpredictable, irritable, and highly sensitive. I constantly feel like I am walking on eggshells around her. Raising a child with ADHD is proving to be very challenging, but what I am realizing is that this "challenge" is making me a better person.

Having a Child with ADHD has Made me More Patient

Parents of children with ADHD need to be given an award for the incredible amount of patience they have with their child. They understand that their child's brain works differently. When I ask my child to put her shoes on and five minutes later, her shoes *still* aren't on because she got distracted by a toy that was next to her shoes for example, I do my best to not lose my temper. I know that she is not a bad kid or a trouble maker. I know she is not deliberately trying to get a rise out of me and make me angry. Like many children with ADHD, my child lives in the moment. All that matters to her is the present, which is actually something I envy about her. I remind myself of this, push the negative words away that were about to come out of my mouth, and practice patience, patience, patience.

Having a Child with ADHD has Made me More Compassionate

There have been countless times my child has had a meltdown in public. Whether it was because she became frustrated with a word search on a children's menu at a restaurant or she was having a hard time waiting her turn to go down the slide at the park,

I have felt the eyes of judgmental parents on my child and me. They may think my child is giving me a hard time, but the truth is my child is *having* a hard time and the rude stares and rolling of their eyes is only making it worse for her. That is a truly awful feeling, so when I am in public and I see a child throwing a tantrum, I never ever judge the parent or the child. I honestly have nothing but compassion and empathy for them, which is something I strive to instill in my child.

Having a Child with ADHD has Made me More Optimistic

Before my child's ADHD diagnosis, she was in a very dark place. At only five years old, she suffered from depression and anxiety, which commonly coexist with ADHD. She constantly said that she wished she were never born and that I deserved a better daughter. When she said those awful words, I felt a pain in my heart like nothing I had ever felt before. She had extremely low self-esteem and would put herself down every chance she got. By educating myself more about ADHD and showing my child compassion, patience, and kindness, as well as getting her the help she needed with medication, behavioral therapy, and the unconditional love and support of her family, she was able to come out of the shadows and see the light in her that I have always known was there. She is now doing very well at school and breezes through her homework most days. She is showing the world she is a superstar in her school plays and has the voice of an angel in our church's children's choir. Words can't express how incredibly proud I am to be her mother and to see how far she has come. As cheesy as it sounds, I know that she can accomplish anything she puts her mind to. No matter what, she will rise to the top and I will always be her biggest fan, cheerleader, supporter, and advocate.

As her mother, I work hard every day to make sure I am doing all I can to provide her with a good life. I make sure she is equipped with all of the right tools to help her succeed and use her ADHD to her advantage. All I really want and what I think all parents want for their children is to have good morals and values. I have been so busy trying to teach my child to be a good person, I never thought that in my thirties, my child would in fact be teaching *me* how to better myself and turn me into a better person. The world has my daughter and her ADHD to thank for that.

i'

A Beautiful Train Wreck

Jessica Jurkovic

WHEN I WAS A LITTLE GIRL, I really thought I was something special. I knew was destined for something huge; that I possessed a natural born greatness that would catapult me into a life of glorious abundance, doing all the important things with all the powerful people.

I don't know how these grandiose delusions came about, but I'm sure that my birth order played a small part in it. As the first child, and with nothing to compare me to, my parents saw my every move as nothing short of amazing. I was literally applauded for performing such feats as throwing my arms above my head when someone asked me how big I was. Fools.

In my early education years, I proved to be quite bright, and breezed through the curriculum, prompting my teachers to identify me as "gifted" and I was offered "enrichment activities" to provide me with more of a challenge. Destined for greatness, I tell ya. I was a shining star.

I don't remember when that light began to fade, but I know that it happened slowly, over many years, like a distant sunset descending into the horizon. I was an impulsive child, and perpetually in motion, two qualities that aren't exactly celebrated in the classroom. I was also forgetful, and completely unorganized, despite my best efforts to keep a neat and tidy workspace like the other kids.

My failed attempts to keep up with the societal expectations of order, punctuality, and the ability to sit still for long periods of time, (any amount of time, come to think of it) took a toll. Teachers grew frustrated with my "refusal" to achieve my full potential, and my parents couldn't understand why I couldn't "just sit still and pay attention."

The tough love approach just perpetuated the downward spiral that became my academic experience. My late or forgotten (or misplaced) assignments resulted in failing grades which just solidified my emerging feelings of self-doubt and disappointment. I began to expect failure and rejection; and because these failures were due to my own careless mistakes, not only did I expect to fail, I believed that I deserved to fail.

I was fifteen years old and a sophomore in high school when I was finally diagnosed with ADHD. My mother suspected as much and a psychiatrist confirmed it. I bought a couple books on the subject, and felt like they were written specifically for me. I felt waves of various emotions. Relief, that I was not alone. That there was an explanation for my struggles with what should have been simple tasks. That there was hope for me. But I could not help but feel a little resentful as well. How much pain and suffering and failure could have been prevented, had I known a few years earlier?

My diagnosis was a turning point in my life and with the help of medication, I was able to shift directions in the path I was headed down, and turned my grades around and eventually went on to become an ER nurse.

While the diagnosis of ADHD has given me an explanation for so much of what I didn't understand about myself, the past experiences leading up to that point had left a sense of worthlessness and inadequacy that was deeply ingrained in my personal identity. All those years of trying to hide what I thought was "defective" about me, had left me feeling like I was a fraud. I was so used to screwing things up and disappointing people, that any success or accomplishment must be some sort of fluke.

When people complimented me, when people congratulated me, when people *liked* me, I just figured I was fooling them. One of those fools happened to be the man I would later call my husband. About ten years ago, in the euphoric, head-over-heels, days of our relationship, this amazing and handsome to-good-to-be-true, was telling *me* how lucky he was to have me. His words must have triggered all of those feelings of inadequacy and worthlessness and drew them to the surface, and I started to sob. Like that inconsolable, puffy-faced, shaking, ugly-cry, kind of sob. And I then I told him...this wasn't real. This whole relationship was a fake. He would never love me if he knew the real me. I'm a train wreck. A failure. I don't even deserve a man of his caliber. It was sad, really, because I really did love him and I never wanted to end things this way.

But what he said next would change my life forever. He looked in my eyes and said, sympathetically, "You are a train wreck, that's for sure... but you aren't fooling *anybody*! But this? Us? There is nothing fake about this. The way I feel when we are together; the way I feel when I look at you? These are very real feelings."

And it hit me. For the first time in as long as I can remember, I felt loved. And I felt deserving of that love. And this life that I had built for myself? My successes, and achievements, and accomplishments. They weren't by chance. And I deserve every single one of them. It was at that moment that I felt the flicker of an old familiar light from somewhere deep within.

·····································

Self-Harm

"*SCARS TELL THE STORY of where you've been. They don't dic-tate where you're going.*"

  - Anon

The Beauty of my Battle Scars

Brianna Miedema

SCARS. WE ALL HAVE THEM. They often tell stories of our childhood, surgeries, and more. However, sometimes scars have a deeper, darker story behind them.

About two years ago, I started harming myself. I knew that what I was doing wasn't normal, but I didn't think there was anything seriously wrong about it. Because I had the mentality that what I was doing wasn't wrong or concerning, I didn't try to cover up the little lines on my arm. I wore short sleeves around the house and didn't think twice about it. Eventually, my mom saw what I had done to my arm and pulled me aside to ask me why I had done it. I was extremely ashamed, and I began to see that what I was doing was something that should be hidden.

After my mom started to notice more things in my behavior that concerned her, she started me in therapy. I wasn't very enthusiastic about going, but I didn't have much of a say in it so I complied. A couple sessions in, I was diagnosed with depression. I had heard of depression before, but I didn't know very much about it. I knew that people with depression were "sad" and that was about it.

As therapy continued, my eyes were opened to many of my thoughts and feelings that were characteristic to depression. Things began to make more sense to me, and I felt like I wasn't alone. I spoke up about a lot of the thoughts I had to my mom, and when my therapist learned of my suicidal thoughts, she recommended that I see a psychiatrist.

I was started on Zoloft, and I really hoped that it would work. However, because I had never been on antidepressants before, I didn't know how they worked. I had heard people call antidepressants "happy pills" so I thought that they would make me happy and give me my life back.

Unfortunately, I was wrong about antidepressants. My condition deteriorated, and I began self-harming again, but I had gotten smarter. I found myself better tools and I became much better at hiding it as well. Many times, I found myself planning to self-harm before I even got home because of situations at school with friends and teachers. Even getting scolded by my parents made me think about self-harming because I was so determined to punish myself for not being good enough. Although I used self-harm as a way to punish myself, it was a punishment I looked forward to.

I tried to get through the summer without anyone noticing the cuts on my legs, and it was very difficult. The weather was warm and I spent a lot of time outside with friends. At some point, they noticed and asked me about them, but I made something up to get them off my back about it. The last thing I wanted was for one of them to find out and tell my parents. I still didn't see anything wrong with what I was doing to myself, so I continued doing it until my parents found out again.

Soon enough, they found out I was self-harming again, and they were disappointed. Not in me, but that's how I read it. It was difficult to accept their help because I felt as if they were angry at me. My mom insisted that she wasn't mad, she was just worried. I eventually accepted their help and worked hard. I stopped self-harming and stayed clean for a couple months. My parents were proud of me, but more importantly, I was proud of myself.

Things in my life seemed to be going uphill. I was dating someone and I felt loved and beautiful. He knew I was depressed and he knew that I had scars, but he didn't care. He loved me just the same.

Our relationship was great, and I loved every second of it but sometimes I found myself worried that he had stopped liking me. These thoughts left me feeling stressed and sad, and to cope—I started self-harming again. Three weeks into our relationship, we broke up. I was completely devastated and the night of the breakup I found myself crying in my bathroom contemplating suicide and clutching onto my blades. It was a hard time for me, and I was so close to doing something drastic, but something inside me told me not to end it all over a boy.

I didn't hurt myself that night, but I hurt myself badly the nights to come. I had ugly, deep cuts in my arms that left the bathroom a mess. My mom found drops of blood on the rug and discussed my condition with the family. They decided to have me assessed for hospitalization at our local inpatient program, but because I wasn't suicidal at the time, I was sent home. They tried to start me on a new regimen of medication, but it almost seemed to make things worse. After being on the meds for a couple months and struggling immensely, I tried to take my own life. I was hospitalized, given new medications and was taught new coping skills, and after a week I was sent home. I returned to the hospital a few months later for self-harm, and was sent home after five days.

Things have gotten better since then. I'm now sixteen and in my junior year of high school. I write blog posts about mental illness to share knowledge in my community and I wear short sleeves frequently. Exposing my scars gives people the opportunity to stare and ask questions, but it's okay because I've made the decision over the course of this journey to not let my scars hold me back.

I've been battling mental illness for a long time, and my scars show that. My scars may seem ugly to others, but to me, they're beautiful. They are my battle scars, and they show my victory.

i'

The True Weight of a Pound

Mary Sukala

TWELVE YEARS OLD. I was draped over a camp chair on a sweltering August day in the backyard, poring through a new chunk of literature that leaped off the shelf at the library: Marya Hornbacher's *Wasted*. A chapter or two in, she speaks of this skinny chick in her skull who forbids her to feast without making some sort of recompense for her grave sin—in this case, vomiting. Skinny Chick vows to release her grip the moment her prisoner becomes the much-coveted *thin*, and I didn't know it yet, but that Skinny Chick walked right into my own skull that day, and she was not going down without a fight. I wolfed down the whole book in only a few sittings, and by the end of it, something in me had changed. Possibly forever.

Thirteen years old. I was changing out of my P.E. clothes in a corner of the locker room. A small group of other barely-pubescents were changing across from me.

"Ugh, why am I so fat?" one of the girls lamented, pinching at her thighs. "I need to lay off the Reese's Pieces. I'm a pig."

"You're not as bad as me," another one piped up. "Last night I ate a whole pint of ice cream. *All by myself.*" She turned to the skinniest youngster in the bunch. "You're, like, perfection. How much do you weigh?"

"Like, eighty-five." There was a certain pride beneath the frankness of her tone.

"Eighty-five?! I'm so jelly!"

Having just been weighed a few days ago by the school nurse, I knew that I was eighty-eight pounds even. My typical carefree, eat-what-I-want-when-I-want-it-self felt almost... gluttonous. I didn't eat lunch the next day or the ones that followed. Pretty soon I was nixing breakfast, too. The moment I got home, I would shove everything in sight down my gullet, fully aware that my stomach would be flat as a board the next day. Ironically, I didn't weigh myself once until the start of the next school year, and when I did, I found that I had, after eating normally around my parents all summer, crept up to ninety-six. I started bingeing out of self-hatred and broke one-hundred within days. I didn't know the true weight of a pound at that point, but if I had to guess, I'm sure it was far heavier than my self-worth.

Fourteen years old. It was the summer before my freshman year. I was bent on slashing that number on the scale to an all-time low. This time was different; more methodical. I would get up bright and early and force my tired body to do Pilates. I tallied every calorie that passed through my teeth. I would then exercise in the afternoon; before I went to bed; and even while I was lying in bed waiting for sleep. I sank down to ninety and I began to love my body for all the wrong reasons.

Sixteen years old. I began making excuses for only eating two pieces of chicken and some Litchi gelatin at the all-you-can-eat Chinese Buffet.

Seventeen years old. I started wasting food for the first time.

Eighteen years old. I was a little more than eighty-four pounds, and no one seemed to notice how much I had disintegrated. The moment my weight started inching toward the mid-nineties, I forced it to plummet back down.

Nineteen years old. I was on my first date with my first boyfriend at the most buttoned up restaurant we can afford. I couldn't get through the meal because I was having too many panic attacks.

Twenty years old. I finally reached rock bottom. Walking home from my boyfriend's place, I started to feel funny about ten minutes into the trek. "Can we stop for a bit?" I asked him, slightly winded. "I don't feel okay." In the weakness of my muscles and the way my vision seemed to fade, it dawned on me: my body is a vessel and I would waste to nothing if I kept this up— definitely not a life will not be worth living. I started to change.

Between the ages of twelve and twenty, eight years, I had been at war with the very nature of myself, and picking up the carnage was not the easiest endeavor. I ate far more than I was comfortable with and avoided the scale even when it seemed necessary. And the anxiety over food was still lurking in the background— a sense of panic still seized me whenever my stomach was full. I had to take a deep breath before I took the first bite of anything, and before I took the second, the third—until the waves of anxiety subsided. I could no longer keep my unhealthy relationship with food hidden anymore, either. My support network, who had always been there for me, stepped up to the plate with unfailing encouragement, love, and patience on the days that were the hardest—the days I thought I would succumb to Skinny Chick once and for all.

Now, a couple months into recovery, I am at a place with food that I haven't known for a long time. I eat what I please and when I'm hungry. Calories are nothing more than arbitrary numbers on the back of a box. Looking back, I can find humor in the time I actually wondered how many calories are in the toothpaste I swallowed or the envelope glue I licked. I am strong, physically and mentally. Maybe I'm not a perfect size zero; maybe I don't have the body of a runway model—but I have known the cost of that body, and I will be the first to tell you that it just doesn't add up.

All these years later, I know the true weight of a pound. And I will tell you: it's absolutely nothing.

i'

....

The Visceral Way
Ashley Lewis Carroll

"PRETZLES." I begrudgingly answered the pediatrician I'd had my whole life when asked me what foods I'd still eat. One word. I was a somewhat stocky sixteen-year-old girl who'd played sports nearly non-stop for the last decade of her life. And yet here I sat.

The doctor left to talk to my mom in the waiting room. When she came back, she looked worried.

"Have you been cutting on yourself?"

There it was. The question I was queasy in anticipation of.

I looked away and nodded.

"Show me."

I pulled up the sleeve covering my right arm to reveal a forearm crisscrossed with self-inflicted wounds. Dried blood on fresh cuts and halfway healed scabs on others. Red and angry and unapologetic. Painful to look at and excruciating to live with. I think

{ 47 }

now about a specific wool sweater with belled sleeves and how the fabric would catch on my scabs and tug. The little realities of being a cutter that so many don't think about. Don't want to.

Tears sprang into my pediatrician's eyes. She looked at my arm and then at me.

"These cuts aren't something I can ignore."

Her words felt like a threat.

"I'll be praying for you."

The follow-up felt like a warning.

I lived life as an on-again-off-again cutter from sixteen until twenty-one. I lived life as an on-again-off-again human through that time also. I was half girl, half woman. Half person, half disorders and diagnoses. Not even half understanding what was even going on with me and how it would influence the trajectory of my life.

When I was sixteen I started starving myself. Then I started binge eating. Then, I started purging. I binged and purged my way through the next six years of life. Because living with an eating disorder sucks, I started self-harming myself to cope. I found I got a brief reprieve from the incessant food thoughts that had so quickly dominated my life. I mostly cut my arms, but also my legs and stomach. I would occasionally branch out into burning and bruising. I even went through a stint of sticking needles in my veins.

I craved the release but hated the harm it did to me. I didn't mean for my arms to become borne with scars that told such a sordid story wearing short sleeves became a political statement.

I wore short sleeves anyway.

I don't always identify as a "cutter." Even though I've spent half my life with cutter scars over large parts of my body. Cutters are scary. Cutters are selfish. Cutters are melodramatic drama queens looking for attention. Or are they? Are cutters maybe the ones holding all the shit in to spare you from the truth? Are cutters the girls who feel too much, love too hard, and hurt so very deeply? Are cutters your favorite people to go to when you have a problem, or need a shoulder to cry on, or that flash of insight you can't quite reach on your own? Cutters are our sensitive souls, walking this world with stories to tell that we've outlined on our skin. Cutting may be scary but cutters are not. We are sad. We are scared. We often feel broken.

I stopped cutting, for the most part, when I started sleeping with my high school boyfriend. To be naked in front of him was hard enough—having fresh cuts made the whole endeavor unbearable. The shame of someone seeing stopped me. The burn of pain reflected in a loved one's eyes. Ouch.

I stopped bingeing and purging when I was twenty-one years old. I was a lost girl at that point. I'd dropped out of college to get treatment. I'd dropped out of treatment when my parents ran out of money. I'd dropped out of life when my parents cut me off and left me alone. Twenty and bulimic. Newly sober and severely depressed. They paid one month's rent at a clean and sober house. No job. No friends. No car. No credit. No back-up plan.

I survived. I put one foot in front of the other. I did the sober thing. I did the not sober thing.

I fell headfirst into a methamphetamine addiction.

I barely made it out.

This is how I made it out: I met a boy. I liked him. By the end of our first date I thought I'd marry him. Just three months after we met I got pregnant with his baby. I got and stayed sober. I learned to eat and not throw my food up. I came back to this thing we call life. I slept and ate and bathed and fought traffic and went to meetings and took classes. I had a baby and built a family. I became a social worker. I became a person.

This is also how I made it out: I took the steps in front of me. I followed directions sometimes. I forged my own path other times. I did the hard work and I took the easy routes. All of it. I learned that life—real life—includes the struggle and the sweet. I learned it the visceral way. Through life.

It's been over decade since I made it out. I still find myself surprised that I did. That life could be good. That people are loving and kind. That skin can heal and scars can flatten and turn white with a whisper. I've found a lot of solace in my story—and a lot of strength in living life while telling it.

I Will Fear No Evil, For Thou Art with Me

Timothy Cyron

I think I'm losing my mind
This demon is within me
It comes from inside

It's been here forever
From it I want to hide
But that's impossible
No matter where I am it finds

Me
We're connected like a bind
It's always hungry
On my sanity it dines

It eats away at me
It won't leave till I die
And that might be soon
My anxiety has arrived

It was over Thanksgiving break in 2015. It was the first Thanksgiving I would spend in my college apartment instead of with my family. My friend and roommate had gone home for the break and I had the whole apartment to myself.

The third night, something I hadn't dealt with in six months occurred. It started subtle, just a dull vibration in the pit of my stomach that slowly got stronger. Soon, my heart began pounding in my chest and was speeding up. Pure adrenaline was now coursing through my veins which made me incredibly alert. It happened so suddenly I didn't realize what it was until I felt fear creeping up inside me telling me I wasn't safe. That was when I realized it was my anxiety.

I needed to calm down, I didn't want to lose control. I closed my eyes, took a deep breath and told myself, "You're fine, take some de—" and then I heard a noise, coming from the other side of the apartment. What was it? I didn't know but I was terrified. Who or what was in my apartment? Had my anxiety been correct in warning me? I was so paranoid, I believed those thoughts. I grabbed a pair of scissors from my desk to defend myself, and backed into a corner. As I stood there petrified, I could feel somebody, or something, watching me.

It's coming back
Stronger than before

It's really scaring me
Banging on my door

My eyes well with tears
I crumble to the floor
My legs start shaking
I can't take it anymore

What's the point of fighting
It fucks me up hardcore
I know it's gonna win
No need to keep score

I let it have its way
Emotionally beats me till I'm sore
When my anxiety attacks
There's gonna be gore

Standing in that corner I kept seeing things out of the corner of my eye. Shadows, and with everyone I saw I got more paranoid, anxious, and afraid. My legs began to shake uncontrollably and I fell to the floor, where all I could do was cry and shake. I couldn't move, or speak, and I was having trouble breathing.

What made all of this worse was that I was alone. Instead of thinking with reason, I was ruled by emotions and it was crippling—like there was no way out. There was still something in my apartment watching me, my heart was beating so fast my chest hurt, I had so much trouble breathing I was worried that I would die.

There had to be something that would calm me down. My Bible? Not right now. Music? No. I would only listen to depressing songs. Maybe I could call or text someone? No. Who wants to listen to me crying, shaking, and incoherent? Desperate, I looked down and saw the scissors...

If I don't do this
I swear I'll go insane
But I wish
I didn't do this again

Pick up the scissors
In my arm find a vein
Close my eyes
Drag my skin across the blade

It hurts so good
Peace of mind I reclaim
My anxiety leaves me
As my blood drains

But it's not fucking worth it
Scars are all I gain
Self-harm doesn't solve it
Just adds to the pain

I picked up the scissors and my only thought was: do it, it will end this anxiety. So, I slashed my left forearm. As my arm began to bleed from the countless cuts, my anxiety began to leave. My breathing returned to normal, my heart rate slowed down. I stopped crying and could speak again. A couple minutes later, I stopped shaking. My anxiety attack ended. Even though I was no longer paranoid I still felt off so I went to the dorm chapel. I lied down on the floor in silence for a couple of hours.

Self-harm unfortunately is still an outlet for me—a way I can release my emotions and calm down. It's not a healthy thing to do, but it helps in the moment. But it becomes addicting. You get a rush of endorphins, which are morphine-like chemicals when you inflict pain upon yourself. There are more productive ways to release your emotions. Exercising, writing, drawing, the alternatives are endless. I'm a work in progress, and there's one more thing that I have found extremely helpful...

When my anxiety
Makes me wanna self-harm
I know there's someone
Who will hold me in his arms

We're his sheep
The earth is his barn
And when the storm comes
We'll be safe in his barn

No matter what
When we raise the alarm
He'll come to our aid
And hold us in his palms

He is the only one

Who can truly keep me calm

His name is the Father

But He cares for us like a mom

Faith is the one thing that keeps me going. For me, it's faith in God, but it could be faith in an ideal, belief, or even yourself. Have faith in something or somebody that you know will be there for you when you're struggling. When I had my anxiety attack, I had lost faith. I didn't think I or my friends or my Bible could do anything to help—and it was then that I lost hope. But faith is something I've had to practice when I'm calm so in situations of anxiety and paranoia I can stay grounded. If you have faith, you'll have hope, and if you have hope, you can make it through just about anything.

....

Suicide

"SUICIDE IS NOT a blot on anyone's name; it is a tragedy."
  - Kay Redfield Jamison

I Survived

Caitlin McLaughlin

2012

I couldn't keep my eyes open. The woman in front of me was fading in and out of my vision as my eyelids drooped. I couldn't feel anything. It was as if I had been dropped in a tub of gelatin, moving in slow motion.

"Last night I wanted to kill myself."

I was sitting in the high school guidance counselor's office, sixteen years old. The night before I had another fight with my friend. Most people don't think about offing themselves because of a teenage fight. Truth is I wanted to kill myself for the last year. I just needed an excuse to say it out loud.

I was constantly reaching for this idea of the perfect person, but I could never achieve it. Living in a two-bedroom apartment where I shared a room with my sister, I was drowning in the circumstances of my life—things I couldn't control.

"And you had a plan?"

I had a plan, a theoretical plan that involved either A.) Jumping in front of a car or B.) Slicing my wrists until I bled out. Killing myself never felt like an action I would complete, but more like a concept I enjoyed pondering at 4 in the morning. Maybe if I lay in bed long enough I'd stop existing.

"I had a plan."

* * *

I was sitting in the corner of the day room, with its fluorescent lighting and concrete walls covered in finger paint. There was a picture of a fish with a big smile on his face, and I wanted to climb into the painting, shut my eyes, and let the waves take me away.

My mind kept traveling back to the night before, when I was first checked into the ward.

I heard it first. Then I saw it. There was a boy with burns all over his body, no ears, and eyes that looked like a skeleton's. He slammed another patient against the wall opposite me, and I jumped back in surprise, as if the skeleton boy would suddenly decide I was his next target. I felt tears prickling behind my eyelids.

I'd only been on the ward thirty minutes, but I felt like I was in hell.

The nurse tapped at her clipboard and wrote something down. I was already told to interact more with the other patients, and the fact that I *couldn't* get myself to do that made me feel like a failure. I couldn't even be a perfect hospital patient.

I was trying to finish *Of Mice and Men*. Lennie had just killed a puppy because he pet it too hard, but I kept crying. I must have cried for at least the first three days of treatment. Sometimes I didn't even know why I was crying.

All I kept thinking was, 'I wish I killed myself,' because I didn't want colleges to find out I was there. I imagined the nurses sending a memo to every college in the country: Caitlin's crazy! Don't admit her!

It had been days since I checked my grades, and I normally checked them once an hour. I couldn't do any of that here. I couldn't calculate my GPA, although I tried once during our 'math class' in the ward.

I vowed that I would kill myself for real next time. I would tell no one. The thought stayed in my mind while I talked to the psychiatrist there.

"One day you're going to be at an Ivy League school with your grades," she said. It was the first positive thing a staff member had said to me on the ward. I told her that I didn't plan to graduate high school. I knew that I'd die before then.

2014

It was the senior award ceremony. I was sitting in my cap and gown that I never thought I'd have a chance to wear. I remember secretly holding out hope that I'd win an award.

Then my favorite teacher, Mrs. Galambos, took the podium to announce the English Department Award. I'd already tuned out at this point. Even though English was my favorite class, I'd always told myself I wasn't any good at it. I was going to college for psychology, because I knew that I couldn't make a career out of writing, even though I loved it.

"This particular student not only cares about equality for the students around her, but is excellent at analyzing literature from a psychological lens."

I knew that she was talking about me—my term paper psychoanalyzed King Claudius in Hamlet, and I repeatedly wrote about my own mental health problems in the class—but when she announced my name, I was still shocked. I was trying not to cry, and I didn't. The tears stayed behind my eyelids. My writings about mental illness meant something to her, and maybe they could mean something to other people.

All the students were surprised. I wasn't the student that was known for excelling in English. But I was validated in that moment for my passion, and suddenly reading *Of Mice and Men* in the psych ward seemed worthwhile. I didn't even think I'd live to graduate high school, and earning that award made me feel like my life meant something.

I write my story so that others struggling with suicidal thoughts know that the world doesn't end just because you seek help. If I killed myself, I'd never have won that award. I'd never get to advocate for mental illness. I wouldn't have gone to college.

You never know just where your life will take you.

The Rainbow After the Storm

Michelle Graffeo

ꓘꓘꓘꓘ

A S FAR BACK AS I CAN REMEMBER I can recall being depressed and always feeling as though I was trapped under a huge dark cloud. Until recently if you asked me ago to give you a happy memory about my childhood I would have found it nearly impossible.

The bad memories come to me in flashes—trying to smother myself with a pillow or drown myself in the bathtub. I was just a child and I was already very familiar with this sense of being different. I had the gargantuan task to hide my overwhelming desire to die. Fear was instilled at a young age, and it poisoned everything it touched. My mother was my only refuge, but there wasn't really much she could do. She had lost custody due to her own mental breakdown, and was leading a lifestyle that only furthered our abusive situation. While living with my father we were being physically and sexually abused. When the sexual abuse ended the physical abuse increased. I was nearly turn thirteen when he hit me for the last time. He not only beat me he humiliated me, and I decided that night that I would give myself two options. Leave in the morning or kill myself. I never came home from school the next day, and it would be twelve years before I would see my Father again. I was placed in the custody of the state until several weeks later when my Mother was summonsed to come and get me.

My first suicide attempt was at the age of sixteen. It was my first true cry for help. It landed me in a respite home, as well as my first trial run with antidepressants. I used to be really critical about the way my mother handled my rage and depression, but I realize now that she was doing the best she could for the small amount of education and information she was receiving from different doctors. I took personality test, analyzed pictures, talked the talk. I wanted so desperately to be normal and to be able to hang with the "in" crowd. But at sixteen my metaphorical resilience and coping toolbox was empty, and so was I. It was only a matter of time before my next suicide attempt. This one happened right after I turned twenty and got mixed up in some pretty hard living. Nothing was off limits but nothing prevented me from feeling empty and hollow. I hid under the dark cloud as long as I could, barely surviving but surviving nonetheless.

The cycle of mania and depression finally got the best of me, and at twenty-seven and I fell apart again. I was growing older, my consequences were growing incrementally, and they began to affect all of those around me. I became toxic, and truly believed I would be doing everyone a favor by dying. I even believed my son would be better off without me. And that led to my third suicide attempt, which I "botched," which then added to my sense of failure. My dark cloud had turned to rain, and there was no getting around it, a storm was coming. It took eight more years, eight hard fought, grueling, relentless years. I did drugs to hide the pain, and I did a lot of them. I did a lot of everything. Honestly, there wasn't much I wouldn't have done. If it made me forget about the shitty mother, person, friend that I had become, then I thought: *bring it!* At thirty-five it all came to an abrupt halt. I can see that day in flashes as well—my fourth attempt at suicide. I thought I was going to die, but for the first time in my life I truly wanted to live.

That was two years and four months ago. In a rare moment of clarity, I realized that it all mattered. And I became completely willing to do whatever it took to not just stay alive, but to truly live. For me, that means owning it, all of it and I'm working towards a life lived with transparency. In June 2014 I became certified with The National Alliance on Mental Illness (NAMI) to lead groups, and in January 2015 I became certified with the State of Louisiana as a Peer Support Specialist. I have also graduated from the BRIDGES program to teach a ten-week course on coping skills and early warning signs, and have my license to facilitate Mary Ellen Copeland's WRAP course on peer-to-peer support. And soon, I will be getting my certification to answer calls on the Warmline (a crisis line in Louisiana). This is what I was meant to do with my life and all of my experiences. Today I know that recovery is possible, and I am here and #iampossible.

i'

Chelsea Did a Backflip
Cynthia Mauzerall

THE NIGHT BEFORE MY BROTHER DIED from suicide he asked me to forgive him for his previous attempt that resulted in a psychiatric hospitalization. He had taken pills and called it an accident. "Don't worry about it," I said. "I'm just so glad you're alive."

He was insistent though and said, "Cyn, you have to forgive me."

I was no stranger to the sensitive and serious side of Dave. He was a Public Defender who represented the Mashantucket Pequot Indians to ensure that when they made money from casinos they were not taken advantage of by lenders or the legal system. One of my earliest memories of Dave's sensitive side was when he felt compelled to tell me there was no Santa at age five because he felt the concept of Santa was wrong in that it made poor children feel like they must be bad if they didn't receive a bounty of gifts Christmas morning.

But something was awry the night before he died—it seemed as if he wasn't so happy to be alive. I swiftly called my sister after the unsettling conversation and we decided together that he just felt remorseful and maybe ashamed. I decided to put my fears and uneasiness aside. Little did I know then that males who come out of a psychiatric hospitalization are more than two hundred fifty times likely to go on to complete suicide in the week after they return home.

The next morning the call came from his wife. My life was forever changed and in that moment and for long after, I was not sure who would understand and terrified of who would judge—not only my brother, but me. One night I woke up and saw our newborn baby's bassinet at the end of our bed. In my sweating, scared and fragile state, I saw a coffin resembling Dave's.

Realizing that he must have been in extreme pain, I found myself doing what many survivors of suicide loss do—I tried to look for clues. I searched endless for evidence of his depression and desperation. One that stuck out for me was his kidney transplant ten years before and the grueling battle of anti-rejection and steroid medications.

A month or so before his death, Dave had seen a doctor who prescribed an antidepressant but it would be trial and error to find something that didn't have counter-indications with anti-rejection medications. I racked my brain to find evidence of a tortured soul who would ultimately die by suicide. I remember my mother and I looking at his artwork on her wall and thinking it seemed a bit dark. An image of him saying his last goodbye and kissing his two-year-old twin boys played through my mind over and over. How could that be?

I secretly loved the fact that I did not have to go back to work as a counselor for six months. After all, how good was I at that role if I failed to help my own brother? I considered other jobs. I would be better at anything other than that right? Once six months passed, I cut myself a deal—I would try my hand back in the field and make an honest assessment of my own ability to help and heal. So, intrepidly off to counseling others I went. What surprise lay in store—I had more compassion, was more willing to ask, willing to hear what is said and not said. I no longer worked a job but found my calling.

As a counselor, I avoid giving advice, but in the role of writer, I can splurge a bit. One simple piece of advice—don't worry about offending. Ask. Ask people if they are in pain of if they are thinking about taking their life. People sometimes ask how Dave would have answered—and I can't be certain. But, I am certain of how it went when I didn't ask. That regret still has power— receding into the basement of my memory but still burns a bit like a dim kerosene lantern.

Beyond finding a renewed love for my calling, another realization arose. A member of my Suicide Survivors Support Group challenged me one day when I was trying to put together the pieces of my brother's struggle and descent into depression. I had shared that my brother was oddly funny right up until his death. Everyone at his wake shared how much they adored his humor. Initially I thought, "How could someone who was so freakin' hilarious die by suicide?" My co-member explained that after the suicide we push away memories of who they were and what other qualities they had. We fixate on sad, depressed, lost.

After that realization, the funny and uplifting memories started flooding in. I could hear him awkwardly yelling, "Chelsea did a backflip!" This most refreshing memory is vivid. I can still hear Dave's stammering impression of Henry Fonda in 1981's "On Golden Pond. We must have watched it twenty-five times as kids. Dave would mimic "Norman" played by Henry Fonda and I would imitate "Chelsea" played by Jane Fonda. Chelsea was always trying to prove herself to her critical father who insinuated she was too chubby to do a backflip. Dave would reel in laughter when I shook my finger at him Chelsea style emphatically stating, "I am gonna do a goddamn backflip!" That funny memory has replaced the old images of him kissing his two-year-old twin boys before he left this world and images of the bassinet morphing into a coffin at night. This has begun to replace the memory of letting him down, failing to see, hear, or ask.

Dave—you were funny, sensitive, and sad. You were a great impersonator, father, husband, son, and brother. You are all these things and always will be.

A Return to Living
Estelle Matranga

IGHT AFTER "IT" HAPPENED, I didn't care which clothes I was wearing, I didn't care to eat and when I did, I didn't care about gaining weight. One is usually pretty self-conscious at twenty-two. I wasn't anymore. I didn't care about the present, I didn't think of the future, there was none anyway. How could there be a day after? I became numb. I was out of myself. Completely.

I went into the utility room where all the family would hang their jackets and vests so they were easy to grab in a rush or so it was close enough to the terrace when the long summer evenings would get chilly. I grabbed my mom's white grainy vest and it became mine for a while. I guess I thought that if I didn't have her arms anymore I should have whatever helped cover hers.

It was the beginning of October, when the days are still nice and warm but the mornings and evenings remind you that soon, the cold will come. This marked the end of the leftover pieces of my childhood, this funny *entre-deux* where you are not a child anymore yet not fully an adult. This, too, was over.

Wednesday, October 6th 2010 was the day during which my mother decided her residency on Earth was over and thereby, the day I was forced into adulthood.

At that time, I had just graduated from college and my flight to visit the United States for the second time was scheduled a week after she passed. The morning after her death, past the long nightmarish *nuit blanche*, the first thing I did was call the airline company I was flying with. I had to either postpone or cancel. To my surprise, I was able to make perfect sense to the lady I was talking to over the phone. Somehow, my brain was functioning.

America had always been a dream of mine. One week before she did it, with my ticket in my pockets, the door and window of my bedroom wide open, I was blasting out the song "L'Amérique" by singer Joe Dassin. From the terrace, she yelled: "You're going to have your America!" She was right—but only much later and in a roundabout way that I could never have imagined. Traveling was such a big deal for me. I had worked a lot and saved for a long time. I was worried I would lose all the money I had spent.

What I realized less than twelve hours after her death—I had to be responsible and figure things out for myself, regardless of the emotional state I was in, and without the comforting idea that she would be there to help me if I needed her to. I was lost in space and time. At a point where all my fellow friends where pursuing their studies or finding their first jobs, I was left with nothing and no hope for a brighter future.

There was one thing that I used to do when mom was still around. Dance. Before I moved to Paris to study Cinema, my mom would get up from the couch late at night to come pick me up from my dance rehearsals. One of the many styles I had been practicing was belly dance. So, in this new land of nothingness after her death, I decided to go back to what had once freed my soul.

Precisely one month after my mom passed, I was on stage with my fellow dancers. I was wearing a beautiful red flowery costume, dancing in a place where joy and deep emotional connection to my inner self would triumph. My mother had always been my number one fan. She was always in the audience capturing my most awkward moments of my youth. That night though, I was more vulnerable and more alive than ever. I couldn't help the tears and I couldn't help the pain. But for the first time, I had hope again.

My life was not over. My life was meant to go on and to be beautiful. I had to keep going, I had to keep doing the things I loved, I had to keep moving. This is how I slowly reengaged with life, by going back to the simple things that used to be a source of joy when she was still around.

I sometimes wonder if I was actually lucky that it happened to me while I was still so young. Youth provides an inevitable thirst for growth and discovery. Youth has dreams. Mine was still alive. So I pursued.

As I grow older, I've discovered the importance of knowing oneself. It takes courage and strength to travel deep within. It means you *will* dive in and face your demons. You will leap into your beautiful disaster and you will come back stronger and more alive than ever. You will get rid of all the self-limiting beliefs you had built upon yourself and you will remember that you are nothing but Love and thus worthy of Love.

There will always be a blurred line in my heart, somewhere between the melancholy and the pride of becoming the woman I am and always have been, thanks to her absence. But my love is stronger and her love for me is still, up to this day, stronger than the pain she was in. *I know this.* So I keep going. I keep dancing. I am becoming the best version of myself. My expansion in Love has, from now on, become limitless.

i

....

Schizophrenia

"*PLEASE HEAR THIS: There are not 'schizophrenics.' There are people with schizophrenia.*"

- Elyn Saks

Garfield, and Bubble Baths, and Schizophrenia; Oh My!

Amy Kay

IN 2005, FRESH OUT OF HIGH SCHOOL, I had my life all planned out and decided to attend a college where I could major in fashion. It was my lifelong dream to work as a lingerie designer. I was following my dreams and sticking to my path—that is, until my junior year of college when everything fell apart.

My euphoric state of mind was quickly changing—a battle between good and evil was being waged, and I was mentally exhausted.

It seemed like everything was a message from God. Shows on the TV. Songs on the radio. Flyers. I felt like God was sending instructions especially for me.

I believed I was Mother Earth and that all souls belonged to me. As guardian of souls I knew the devil was ruling the earth—and I was on a mission to take back all of my children.

On one particularly harrowing day, I was home with my one of my best friend's Grandma. I became convinced that Grandma was possessed with a demon. I took my Bible and tried to press it to her face to get rid of the demon. Needless to say she locked me out of her room—and I don't blame her.

Soon after my failed exorcism of Grandma, I walked for several hours to a popular mega church. I thought the pastor was the devil in disguise—and I was ready for a showdown of Biblical proportions.

It was getting dark outside and nobody was there. I walked around the church looking for a way in but all of the doors were locked. I spent the night outside at the church waiting for something, anything, to happen. I was hoping all souls on Earth would return to me, so I started reading the Bible out loud until I fell asleep.

The next morning, I returned to my best friend's house, determined as ever. I knocked on the door but no one answered. I had to complete my mission from God, so I broke in through a window.

My best friend, scared and confused, had my brother come to the house so they could both try to calm me down.

"You are not my brother and you are not best friend," I shouted. "You are clones trying to kill me!" Somehow, I broke free from their grip and dashed off down the street with the two of them chasing me through neighborhood yards.

After successfully ditching my brother and friend, a police officer stopped me and she began to ask me questions. "You don't understand! My older brother and my best friend are trying to poison me," I explained.

"What's in your purse?" the officer asked. The look on her face suggested she thought I was on drugs. But all I had in there was my Bible and a few pieces of candy.

The next thing I know, the officer and her partner put me in the backseat of their cruiser and drove me to the hospital. I was escorted to a room with a bed where a doctor came in to check on me. He had an evil look in his eyes, so I took my Bible and tried to press it against his face. Another failed exorcism was enough for them to strap me to the bed and give me a shot.

Soon after, they escorted me to the mental ward. "I am God!" one of the patients screamed.

I. Am. Eve," said another patient. "I am the first lady created by God. And there are a few dead people following you," she told me.

"Leave me alone, dead people," I cried, wishing I could wave my Bible in their direction.

Everyone in the mental ward seemed so... normal to me.

As soon as my parents and little brother got wind of what I was going through, they hopped in a car and drove eight hours from Mobile, Alabama to Orlando, Florida to take me home with them.

At this point I was still a bit delusional but more stable than the few preceding days. After being discharged from the hospital, my older brother, best friend, and two close friends came to help me pack my things. I was only slightly sad to say goodbye to my friends because I thought my move would be temporary. I was certain that after I got better I would be back in Orlando after a few months.

But as soon as I got to Mobile, my doctors told me that I had indeed had my first psychiatric breakdown. The doctors diagnosed me with schizophrenia and without proper treatment, my mental illness would slowly take over and control my mind, just as it had before I left Orlando.

I followed doctor's orders and lived in a group home for two months. But my dad realized how miserable I was and had me discharged. I was ecstatic when I left the group home! I was free and I was home again with my family. I never wanted to go back to that home again so I learned to develop coping skills—spending time with friends, listening to relaxing music, bubble baths, and even petting my sweet cat, Garfield; just to name a few.

Life has changed dramatically since being released from that awful group home. For the past two years, I have served on the board of a mental health organization and I am also on the Consumer Council of a local mental health place. I have a blog on my journey living with schizophrenia that has been published in numerous places and read in several countries. I am a facilitator for Schizophrenia Alliance. I have given various speeches to colleges and the police department. I will continue on in my efforts in mental health advocacy, erasing the stigma, and making sure people have access to the help they need and deserve.

Discerning the Truth
Victoria Marie Alonso

DURING 2006 AND 2007, the messages came to me clearly and frequently, no two alike but similar in nature. It wasn't necessarily a voice but a strong thought that I had to obey. If I didn't, terrible things would happen, like I would become crippled and unable to move causing a scene, which was against everything that I stood for. No drama was my mantra, but I was becoming increasingly dramatic with all that I had to do for God. Other times it was a strong compulsion and the thought would repeat, growing stronger each time I didn't do as it wished.

I was on a very special mission—to save the Church one priest at a time. And it was not an easy task because they often ignored my demands to do things right, traditional, exacting commands. The letters poured forth and I delivered them at the time I was

{ 81 }

told. But things weren't working out as planned and I was getting in trouble from the people I was trying to help via the many messages. I believed I was a prophet but nobody except a few believed me.

I was exhausted at the end of every day and often stayed up at night to write more letters, some through email. I would also receive commands for the next day although the commands came throughout the day too, but they were stronger at night when I was alone. They also came when I was driving while I was praying and one time I clearly heard the voice of Jesus. Another time very distinctly heard the voice of Mary encouraging me on my mission.

My duties as a wife and mother were secondary to the many tasks I was asked to perform for God and it was getting hard to focus on anything except the commands. I should have seen this as a red flag, but when one suffers from a mental disorder, insight into behavior is often lacking which is another symptom of having a disorder.

By 2008, when things weren't working out with my mission, I knew something was wrong with my mind. So I researched online and came up with the diagnosis: schizophrenia. I knew I desperately needed help. My life was falling apart and anyone who God told me to reveal a message to would become worried about me and my "mission." When my mission began to interfere with my functioning level I decided to get help.

Things were happening around me all the time and it all was signs from God. When the wind blew strong I knew God was mad at someone for denying his will. When the signal lights changed for me or when God told me to follow the ambulance to get to my destination quicker, I became puzzled at these strange happenings.

I finally got myself into a mental hospital on a hold because I believed I could stop traffic and watch the angels of God rescue me from harm. I was a danger to myself and was scared as were my parents. My parents drove me to the hospital and the hospital accepted me stating that I did not have schizophrenia because I was too old for this kind of diagnosis among other factors.

Within three days I was diagnosed by a team of doctors at UCLA to conclude what I suspected—I had schizophrenia. Soon after, my psychiatrist fine-tuned it to schizoaffective disorder due to bouts of serious suicidal depression. The medicine stopped all the messages and I haven't heard a voice in over eight years. I still believe in God and rarely will he give me a message or task but I can ignore it easily if I choose. If I think it worthwhile, I check in with my adult daughter, who has been my main support.

There have been ups and downs during the last eight years, but today I virtually live symptom free from the psychosis, however am still affected by the negative symptoms. Post diagnosis I earned my Masters' degree in psychology and worked in the mental health field for four years. The work I did was very rewarding, but it ended up being too stressful on my mental health and I had to go on permanent disability. And even though I am not working I have found fulfillment in my life. Most days I don't miss working because I am busy with many worthwhile activities such as spending time with my three awesome children, my husband who has stood by me through it all, my elderly parents and friends. I now have time for gardening, hiking, walking, exercising, cleaning house, cooking healthy meals and fun DIY projects. I have also written a few books; one of them is called *My Personal Recovery From Schizophrenia*.

I still have rough days but they happen less frequently and if I have several in a row I see my psychiatrist sooner than planned and discuss medication management and my triggers. Stress for me is the worst thing and has brought on several relapses, so I avoid it at all costs.

I have learned many things through this never-ending journey of recovery, one being that I am limited in the work I do, but I can still make a positive difference in this crazy world. I have many gifts and they did not go away because I have a disorder. I am able to take care of my elderly parents and others and if I ever run out of family and friends to help I will definitely volunteer somewhere. Life does not end when one has a mental disorder—it is only the beginning!

i

·······································

Thawed
Bethany Yeiser

WHEN I LOOK OUT the window of my apartment, I see a church building with tall, stone pillars. The dark, wooden front doors are beautiful. But with a careful look, a crack in the glass of a church window becomes visible. It has been mended with tape.

I first noticed the vacant church building when I moved to the University of Cincinnati neighborhood several years ago. I passed the scrubby lawn with its overgrown bushes every time I walked to my university classes. I hoped the church would reopen. But instead, the front sign was removed, leaving only a foundation with empty screws, and the doors were all locked.

One day, out of curiosity, I pressed my face against a side door. Through the glass, I could see the edge of the sanctuary, carpeted in a subtle olive green. Matching, padded, empty pews were positioned in rows, facing a stage. As I looked inside, I was knocked back to a different time and place, when I experienced a deep dormancy inside myself.

There was a time when I was unable to maintain relationships, and I no longer had academic dreams or ambitions. My heart felt icy cold inside of me. I had lost interest in playing my violin in churches and with orchestras, which had once been a source of joy. Undiagnosed schizophrenia had become a silent but devastating intruder.

Violin had always been my passion. At thirteen, I became a violinist in the Cleveland Orchestra Youth Orchestra, and performed in Cleveland's Severance Hall, with its marble floors and tall pillars. I also played violin in a church, for weddings and services, in front of a shining stained glass cross.

I chose biology as my college major, and I also served as concertmaster of the university community orchestra. In my spare time, I performed with companies that recorded music for commercials. My second, less expensive violin accompanied me to Nairobi, Kenya in Africa, the summer after my junior year of college. I volunteered there and performed for Kenyan friends.

After returning to America and settling into my dorm room for the fall, my life plans radically changed. Suddenly, I could not read normally. I struggled to concentrate, and was unable to take meaningful notes during class lectures. I felt an irrational and overwhelming sense of obligation to do something about the poverty I had seen in Africa.

As I rejected help from family and friends, my violin remained untouched and forgotten in its case. I refused to correspond with people who cared deeply about me, who I thought I still loved. I quickly sold my violin to a dealer, for an absurdly low price, and sent the money to a medical project in Africa.

While putting my violin up for sale, I felt an emptiness inside that was almost tangible. I felt no guilt for ignoring all communication from family and friends, and no regret over selling the violin. I did not feel angry, or confused, or upset. When friends and family members wrote me again and again, I did not even feel a sense of annoyance, as I blocked their messages, almost mechanically, from my email account.

I rarely remembered the excitement I felt doing research in college, or the pleasure I experienced when I played the violin. It was as though all my relationships, ambitions, and dreams had momentarily disappeared, or were frozen in time. It began in fall of my senior year, when I was first unable to study.

Four years later, when I was hospitalized for schizophrenia, I was resistant to beginning treatment, unaware of how the illness had altered the course of my life. But after a few days on medication, I began to feel emotions I had not perceived in years. I wanted to see my parents again, and relatives, and friends. I wanted to know what had happened in their lives, while I was "away."

I also wanted to play my violin again. When I realized I sold my best violin, it felt like I had lost a best friend, and I was devastated.

Doctors said that a full recovery was probably not possible. But after a family friend gave me a violin as a gift, I found that my fingers remembered much of their skill. I began to play the violin with other musicians for church services. Violin served as a way to remember who I was, and what was important to me. Through playing, I had a gift to share.

After two years in treatment, with medication and the support of family and doctors, I regained most of my musical ability. I transferred to the University of Cincinnati to finish my bachelor's degree, and graduated two years later. Thanks to treatment, my heart warmed, and my life moved on.

Every Thanksgiving and Christmas, I play classical and religious violin music for the homeless and working poor, at dinners sponsored by a local Cincinnati church. When dinner is over and I leave, I often see homeless people resting outside in dirty sleeping bags. Many of these people are severely mentally ill, and I know the sense of emptiness some of them experience. I hope that the struggling people who hear the violin will one day find the medical treatment they need, so they might also awaken from the empty feelings of dormancy, sometimes associated with schizophrenia, and other mental illnesses.

I wish I could take my violin into the empty church, tune it, and listen to it resonate, bringing music to the sanctuary, after many years of silence. The abandoned church building always reminds me of my own empty, difficult years. I hope that someday the church will be filled with friends, laughter, and music again.

Today, I have ambitions, dreams, and meaningful relationships. I am grateful to the doctors, family members, and friends who have helped me to finally move on. When I play my beautiful violin, it brings healing and warmth into my heart.

i

....

A Schizophrenic's Secret World

August Pfizenmayer

ROM A YOUNG AGE, I believed there were people all around me trying to kill me and my family. They hid in the walls of my house and sat folded up behind the kitchen cabinets. Dying children reached out to me to save them and big scary men chased me with hatchets. Even Jack Nicholson had it out for me, following me to the bus stop or through the park on a sunny day. I was never safe. This was my life. I didn't know any better. I thought I was special with responsibilities that no one else had. It was always up to me to save the world. I would tap my teeth together or count as high as I could until the holes in the sky closed back and the universe felt right again. The world was so fragile. It was exhausting and exhilarating to take care of it.

I sensed that something was different about me, but I did not know how to explain what I did not understand myself. Sometimes, I thought I was actually dead, that my own body was an illusion. I didn't know how to explain that I did not merely feel dead inside, but actually believed I was nonexistent. My parents said I thought too much. My friends said I had a wild imagination. I began to realize that no one was ever going to take me seriously, so I scribbled on silent pages that asked no questions, allowing me to talk about my strange experiences without having to explain them. I could barely keep up with my secret world, and I learned to hide my fear and frustration behind anger. I was a sad child, a moody teenager, and finally, an angry adult. But why?

The only thing I was sure of was that I needed to keep it all a secret. I hid my world, all of it. Even when I was sure there was a murderer standing behind me with an axe, I smiled anxiously at my teachers and peers. I was taught that appearances matter most, and if I could not explain my pain and confusion, then I was not allowed to express it. I would still be hiding it all if I had not crumbled my sophomore year in college. Saving myself and the world from death and destruction was too hard when I was trying to build a life in the real world. Which threats were real and which were not? I ended up in the hospital when I could no longer determine the answer to that question.

Stuck in a building with scheduled snack times and screaming patients, I spent most of my time looking out the window. It wasn't until I no longer had access to the real world that I realized I wanted to be a part of it. But how? I was experiencing psychosis and could not trust my own senses, my own thoughts. I had to do exactly what the delusions and paranoia told me not to.

I had to trust others, leaning on them for reality. I had to believe them when they told me the medication would help me. I had to trust the cardboard cut-outs and imposters when they told me they were real and that I was safe. I could see demons all around me, but my eyes deceived me. I smelled rotting flesh, tasted blood and dirt in my mouth as if I'd eaten my way out of a grave. I saw and felt spiders crawl all over me. It took all my willpower to remain calm. And I would tell myself that I was some sort of god, that I could travel through time and space. It was all up to me to keep everyone safe from the dangers that only I could see. But now I have to trust others when they tell me that my mind lies to me.

Returning to reality and rebuilding my life began in the hospital when it became clear to me that I was not getting out as quickly as I wanted. I hit rock bottom, and there was nowhere to go besides up. I looked at my roommate who had been talking to herself all morning. I told myself that I wasn't better than her or anyone else, that I must try. When I finally chimed in on one of her monologues, her face lit up. A friendship was born.

I often felt like I was trapped inside a snowglobe, watching everyone else live out in the real world. Being diagnosed with schizophrenia shattered that illusion. It was up to me to reach out and reconnect with the world around me. I had to *want* to get better, to try different medications and new ways of thinking. I had to give people a chance. I had to trust the world that I thought was out to get me for so long. I still have doubts, but every day I wake up and make a conscious decision to trust the people around me... and it has gotten me this far.

Posttraumatic Stress Disorder

"AFTER A TRAUMATIC experience, the human system of self-preservation seems to go on permanent alert, as if the danger might return at any moment."

  - Judith Lewis Herman

i

···

How PTSD Became my Beautiful Detour

Amy Oestreicher

GREW UP THINKING AN ILLNESS was a cold or a fever. At eighteen years old, "illness" took on an entirely different meaning. Illness meant waking up from a coma, learning that my stomach exploded, I had no digestive system, and I was to be stabilized with IV nutrition until surgeons could figure out how to put me back together again. Illness meant a life forever out of my control and a body I didn't recognize.

I was shocked and saddened that I could never get my old body back. But what really startled me was realizing what had happened to my mind. Not only had I woken up in a new body, I was now troubled with anxious thoughts, associations, and memories—PTSD.

When a blood clot caused my body to go into septic shock, my life changed forever, and I spent the rest of my senior year in a coma. I had this fantasy that the day I was finally discharged from the hospital, everything would be "back to normal." I'd have my old body back and I'd be eating and drinking again. I'd be nimble like I was in dance class just the week before my coma. These surgeries would just be a "blip" in my life, and now it could proceed as it was meant to.

I waited for the day I could finally eat again, which came after a nineteen-hour surgery requiring three shifts of nurses and doctors. I would finally feel like me again. Eating food made me feel again, but it also made me remember, even the things I didn't want to remember, things that I thought a coma had permanently repressed... including having been sexually abused by my voice teacher, also my godfather, for months before all this.

Staying out of my body and dissociating was how I coped with memories of sexual abuse and medical traumas. Feeling tormented by flashbacks. I was extremely anxious and spent years disassociating. If I couldn't constantly fidget or find another way to "numb out" I would start to panic, and would be overwhelmed with even more memories and raw, forgotten emotions. My anger would end up being misdirected at others, when really I just wanted to shout at my circumstances. My anxiety manifested in all the wrong places—I couldn't sit still in classes and couldn't function as a calm, responsible adult. Soon, these symptoms were controlling my life.

PTSD is something I still struggle with because my traumas happened to me, they have affected me, and will always be a part of me. But I've learned how to thrive in spite of what happened to me and for the first time, my life feels bigger than my past. I've found healthier ways to cope.

The PTSD term for finding healthy coping skills is "self-soothing." To live a healthy thriving life, I've had to befriend my past, embrace my experience, and express what had happened to me. I needed to tell my story in order to heal. But first, I had to hear my story for myself, rather than avoid it. Once I learned how to hear my own heart-shattering story, and feel the pain, the frustration, the anger, and ultimately, the gratitude, I was able to speak to it. I was able to gently teach myself how to live in the present rather than in the world of the trauma.

Healing didn't come all at once. Every day I tried to face a memory a bit more. I called it "dipping my toes" in my trauma. Finally, I could put words to my grief. I was able to write, "I am hurting."

Once expression helped me face my own story, I was able to share it. I wrote a one-woman musical about my life, *Gutless and Grateful,* and started touring it as a mental health and sexual assault prevention program all over the United States. And the day I first shared my story with someone else, I realized I wasn't alone—other people had been through trauma also. Being able to share my story emboldened me with a newfound strength and the knowledge that terrible things happen, and if other people can bounce back, then so can I.

Over a decade has passed since my life took an unexpected detour that put most of my life plans on hold. But this detour turned into the richest time in my life. To this day, I am *still* healing. Every morning I make a new attempt to find who I am and to discover who I am becoming. If I had waited for life to be "perfect," or to go back to "how it was," I would have missed out on a lot. I would have never mounted my first solo art show after learning to paint in the hospital, or written a one-woman musical about my life that I've performed for five years, or given a TEDx talk. If I hadn't had the audacity to set up an online dating profile for myself while still in my hospital gown, recovering from a disastrous surgery, I would never have married the first love of my life. And when I was suddenly hit with a divorce less than a year later, I learned that there is never a reason to wait to fully love yourself.

Every day is an opportunity to learn, to grow, and better myself. I love the imperfect twists and turns my life has taken, simply because they have made me who I am.

I've learned that illness isn't always in the physical scars—that some wounds aren't visible, and some wounds even we don't know we have, until we choose to take care of them. But I've also learned that I'm resilient, strong, broken and put together again, differently, yet even more beautiful—like a mosaic.

PTSD has not broken me. It's taken me apart, and I'm reassembling myself day-by-day. In the meantime, I'm learning to love what I can build.

It Took Me Over Forty Years to Find my Calling... And it was Worth it

Matt Pappas

A S A YOUNG CHILD, I had this vision of what my life would be like as an adult from my twenties all the way through retirement. I would graduate high school, go to college, be a marine biologist, get married, have the two-and-a-half kids, a dog, and a cat. We would vacation every summer, have a nice house, two nice cars, I'm sure you know how it goes.

But all too often life doesn't turn out the way we envision it. Our hopes and dreams change from the career, family, and white picket fence, to just surviving the day ahead.

Between the ages of five and ten, all I could manage was survival—making it from one day to the next while enduring sexual abuse at the hands of a family friend. And little did I know that the lasting effects were just beginning to manifest themselves.

I suppressed my trauma for over thirty years; instead opting for what I thought was the most "life" left I could figure out. I got married, had two incredible kids, but within five years that married ended in divorce.

After spiraling out of control and drowning my sorrows in alcohol, I began to put my life back together. Or so I thought. I got married for a second time and along came my third child (who is also incredible).

After twelve years of struggling financially and with insecurities that I never connected to my past, my second marriage also ended. I was a twice divorced, father of three—forty-one years old and literally hanging on by an emotional thread. Every. Single. Day.

I immediately went into survival mode, and tried to live my life as best as I could. Spending time with my kids, going to work, trying not to think too much about the way my life had unfolded to date. I was just existing and nothing more.

But in January 2015, I had had enough of treading water—something had to change. I utilized a benefit at my job and got hooked up with a therapist as a last ditch effort to try and put my life on track. Notice I did not say, "back on track," because looking back I was most definitely never on track at all.

I admit I was fortunate to find an amazing professional to work with. After my first consultation I knew we were on to something that was going to be beneficial to my life.

The first six months or so were spent mainly working through the hardships of divorce. That transitioned into the inevitable—working through my abuse, and the beginning of my life changing experience.

Throughout the remainder of the year we would dive into every bit of the sexual abuse that I experienced at the hands of the family friend and neighbor up the street, as well as the invalidation and emotional abuse from my mother. We worked on numerous things like mindfulness, writing a letter to my abuser, and learning why the abuse wasn't my fault.

That last statement is a big one. As a victim, I blame myself quite extensively for what happened to me. "Why didn't I just run away?" "Why didn't I tell someone what was happening?" These types of thoughts haunted me well into the coming year and still to today.

Although I continue to work though where the blame really lies—with the perpetrator—I still have progress to make. As I continue this healing journey, I'm discovering more and more about myself. When you dive deep into your past, put in the hard work to understand it—and as my good friend and coach, Athena Moberg says "Feel all of your Feels"—you can gradually begin to put the pieces of your life together.

As survivors, we are puzzle solvers. Our minds are constantly trying to figure out where all the missing pieces have gone, what caused them to vanish, and then make sense of them as we rebuild our lives into something we can look forward too instead of dread.

In an effort to deal with the roller coaster of emotions, thoughts, anxiety spikes, depression, flashbacks, and dissociative episodes, I decided to start journaling. As I did this for a couple months I began to see the cathartic and therapeutic benefits of writing. I then decided to start my blog, "Surviving My Past."

Initially I wrote it as a therapy blog to deal with life in between weekly sessions, but it quickly morphed into something bigger than I anticipated. In a short period of time I began to see just how validating my stories and struggles with daily life are for so many other survivors.

I reached out and joined weekly survivor groups online in which we chat, share, and support one another. That lead to becoming heavily involved with Trauma Recovery University, founded by Athena Moberg and Bobbi Parish. Two women, survivors themselves, who have devoted their life to supporting and educating survivors of abuse.

It took me more than forty years to arrive at the revelation of what I was meant to do with my life. I know now that helping other survivors is my calling. I have been through, first hand, the trauma that millions have been experienced. I know what it's like to be abused, to have a narcissistic parent, to have no self-esteem, no confidence, social anxiety, depression, and I want to use that to educate, inspire, and validate as many as possible.

I know that I can make a difference, to let others know that they are not alone, and that there is hope. Healing is possible. Living the life we desire and deserve is possible.

Adopting a New Mindset, and Learning to Love Myself

Karen Strait

M Y LIFE BEGAN AS Helen Marie Fisher, but my three older brothers and I were taken from our home somewhere around the time I was six months old due to neglect. At twenty-two months, I was adopted by a family who changed my name to Karen Kay Cashen. My new parents already had a boy who they adopted as well. As I grew into a toddler, I craved love from my new family but could never find it.

My adoptive mom would often yell at me or slap me across the face, which would cause me to cry. "Stop being such a cry baby," she would say, relishing the chance to taunt me. Her mom, my adoptive grandmother, lived with us until she passed away when I was in first grade. She was a sweet woman who would often give me a penny to stop crying. After my grandmother died, my mom would often threaten to send me back to the orphanage. One day she packed a suitcase, shoved it in my hand, and made me stand outside. I stood on the porch and cried my heart out until my father came home and took me inside.

I loved my adoptive father. He would chase me in the yard and sometimes he would play catch with me. But he was an alcoholic, who often saw came home staggering and slurring his words. When my mom went to work, he would take me with him to the bar. On Friday nights, we often ate our dinner there. Thankfully when I was a freshman in high school, he stopped drinking after being in a bad car accident.

My father had a cousin, Carl, who owned a shoe repair shop very close to our home. When I was seven, my mom began sending me there to drop off or pick up shoes. Carl had a rocking chair that he would rock me in, and I loved the attention. Eventually he started engaging in inappropriate behavior with me, but at that age I didn't really know what was happening. For three years this went on, and told me to never tell my parents. After seeing him, he always gave me money or candy or stuffed animals. Then one day he shoved me into his closet and went further with me than ever before. Fortunately, my brother came looking for me and my parents found out.

At that point my mother's behavior grew worse. "You are never to tell anyone what happened with Carl, she said and then looked me in the eyes, "You are now dirty." She was constantly finding ways to punish me—even for things my brother did, and it seemed as if she enjoyed verbally abusing me and breaking me down. Every time I tried to succeed, I could hear my mother's hateful voice.

Through high school, I began to totally see myself as a failure and unlovable. My depression grew. And I struggled with why not one but two mothers rejected me. I loved my adoptive mother and would do anything for her, but anything I did was never good enough for her, not even the husband I chose—a kind man and a pastor.

I thought marriage would fix everything, but it didn't and my self-esteem suffered. Because I was sexually molested, I couldn't enjoy intimacy with my husband—for me it was based around the feeling of obligation. I couldn't understand how one piece of paper stating that you were married suddenly made sex okay. I wasn't happy and on Sunday mornings, I would go to church and put on the smile of a happy, perfect pastor's wife.

I desperately wanted children and was thrilled when both of my boys were born. But after the birth, I had to have a hysterectomy and once again, I felt I was a failure, less than, an incomplete woman. My mother even found a way to capitalize on one of the darkest periods of my life by sending me hateful letters. The one that stood out the most was when she wrote, "I am embarrassed to be seen with you."

As my sons grew, my self-esteem diminished further. My oldest son, a counselor, encouraged me to go back to college. I always wanted an education and to help people. So I went back but was very unsure of myself and had a hard time seeing over the metaphorical walls I had built around myself.

But two years later, I finished my bachelor's program with a double major in psychology and sociology. I even made the Dean's list by getting straight A's. I wasn't sure what to do next, but then my son once again encouraged me, and I decided to go for my master's degree in counseling. I took on that challenge and brick by brick, I slowly broke down the walls that had kept me trapped for years. I graduated with all A's and one B.

While going to college, I learned that I struggle with posttraumatic stress disorder (PTSD) and by facing this trauma, I have learned I can handle most anything.

All these years later, I still have many goals in my life to complete. My joy comes from helping people deal with grief and helping to promote suicide prevention. I know now that I can climb mountains with my faith in God and all I have learned, both through my traumatic childhood and by raising two boys. I want others to believe in themselves, to tap into the incredible power inside themselves, and to know that it's possible to not only survive the horrific things that life throws your way—you can thrive as well.

Healing Through Giving

Candace Yoder

A SIREN. A ZIP-TIE. A pistol. A knife. A male figure walking in the shadows after dusk. All triggers for post-traumatic stress (PTSD)—my brain telling me to fight or flee when my senses are overloaded with reminders of one of the worst days of my life.

October 5th, 2015 was a "normal" day like so many others. I woke my kids, made their lunches, and got them off to school. "Normal" mom stuff. I took my time getting to work that day because my mom was visiting us from out of state and I wanted to spend as much time as I could with her. "Normal" daughter stuff.

Not long into my work day, I got a call from a number with the same area code of the town where my father lived. My father was a bit of a loner—my parents had been split up for more than twenty years—and my thoughts raced as my phone rang.

Ring.

He must have fallen down the stairs because of his bad back.

Ring.

What if he took his life? All the time he spent alone—it didn't seem healthy.

Ring.

Could he have gotten arrested? But for what?

Nothing in my wildest imagination could have prepared me for what I heard from the police officer on the other line. As soon as the words left his mouth, my body collapsed to the floor, my heart erupted in terrible emotional pain, and I cried uncontrollably— not for days or weeks but for months, mostly in secret. No one could know the true nature of what I was feeling.

The man on the other line said, "Death. Probably foul play."

Murder? My father? But how? Why? This wasn't fair. This wasn't "normal."

Unfortunately, homicide is all too normal for more than 14,000 people in the U.S. every year along with their friends and families. My father was one of those unlucky 14,000 and I was now in a club no one wanted to join.

My brain would never be the same, forever altered by the trauma I experienced—not just because of my father's death but the fallout that nearly tore my family apart. Each of my children's grief manifested in different ways: night terrors, isolation, a drop in their school work, and even placing the blame on me, their mom.

I had worked hard for over eighteen years as a single mother to provide for my children, for my family, to make sure they wanted for nothing and that they had all the emotional support and love they could ever wish for. But now their grampa's murder threatened to destroy me and us.

In the aftermath, my brain felt like it was enveloped in a never ending fog. I couldn't remember simple tasks, I had little will to get any work done for my job or even around the house, and little things would set me off: A siren. A zip-tie. A pistol. A knife. A male figure walking in the shadows after dusk.

With intensive therapy I was learning to manage symptoms of my PTSD but the pain and the fear and the intrusive thoughts about my father wouldn't completely subside. But over the course of the following summer, I started to feel a bit like my old self and much lighter—until the detectives working my father's case made a major find and caught the people responsible for his murder.

Waves of grief, anger, desperation, and hopelessness washed over me and I was set back to the day I found out my father had been taken from me. From that point I made it a point to go to every hearing and every preliminary trial, learning things about the severity of his murder and all the brutal things my father had experienced right before he died.

After the judge set a trial date to hear my father's case, I knew I had to be in that courtroom every single day to represent my father, to make sure that everyone knew that he was loved and cared for and not just another statistic. I didn't care about the two-hour flight and the additional two-hour drive or the three days each week I'd have to sit in a courtroom—in the long run it would be worth it.

But I knew that I couldn't help my father or his case if I wasn't helping myself. The fog in my brain wasn't lifting and I had to work even harder to have a clear head and manage the symptoms of my PTSD that were seemingly not getting better. So, I doubled down with my therapist appointments and I even saw a psychiatrist who prescribed me medicine that began to work.

It's only been a few months since my father's trial date was set but I have tools to lessen the severity of my PTSD: a great therapist, effective medicine, an incredible support system, and the will to want to work as hard as I can to heal.

Now, I'm speaking in prisons and juvenile detention centers, hoping that my story might keep just one person from making the same mistakes as the five men who murdered my father. It's also my hope that through my efforts, I can help families heal—whatever that means to them—and provide support to families who are survivors of their loved one's homicide. Nothing I do will change the past, bring my father back, or completely close the gaping wound that cut my soul in two. But focusing on others helps ease my pain a bit, which means that not only #iampossible, but #werpossible ... together.

Borderline Personality Disorder

"PEOPLE WITH BPD are like people with 3rd degree burns over 90% of their bodies. Lacking emotional skin, they feel agony at the slightest touch or movement."
  - Marsha M. Linehan

Dear Self

Danielle Hark

DEAR SELF...

If you are reading this, then you have fallen into that void of darkness once again. You're feeling sad, anxious, scared, alone. You don't understand what is happening or why. You are probably in bed right now not knowing when the last time you left the house was, or when you last showered or changed your clothes. Your thoughts are spiraling down a negative path, and your cheeks are stained with tears. Or even worse, you are numb to emotions.

But listen to me...

I know you're feeling like a horrible wife, friend, daughter, and human—but you're doing the best you can right now, and your friends and family love you no matter how badly you feel. I know it's hard to believe, but they do. If they don't, they're not worth your energy. Stop telling yourself you're a bad mom. You're not perfect, that's for sure, but no one is. Your kids are beautiful, bright, and happy. They deserve to have you in their lives for many years. They love you. They need you. They are not better off without you.

You are a worthy human being. You have helped countless other people struggling just as you are struggling right now. They have gotten through it, and you will too. I can vouch for that.

Tell yourself what you tell others who are struggling...

Bring yourself to the present moment. Use your senses. See the beauty in the world around you. Distract yourself. Watch a funny show. Create. Take photos. You love taking photos, even in your room. Meditate. Be around other people who empathize or care. There are people in your life who love you and want to support you. Let them be there. Use them for a nice conversation or even a silent hug. They won't care what you look like or how shitty you feel. Your dog is good for that too. Use your online supports, like Broken Light Collective. Share your story and photos, or view those from others who have been there and are now in a better place. Do the opposite of whatever you want to do right now that is negative—which is probably pretty much everything. If your mind is stuck in the darkness... find the light. Find something positive to focus on, no matter how small. If you want to hurt yourself... hug yourself. It doesn't have to be an actual hug (I see you rolling your eyes), but find a way to do something caring for you. You may think that self-harmful behavior will make you feel better, but in the long run it will not.

If nothing else, it will lead to more feelings of shame and guilt, which is pretty much the last thing you need right now. If you want to stay in bed all day... Get. Your. Ass. Up. Take a walk. Bring your camera. Even a brief walk to the end of the block is a step in the right direction. Opposite action works. Above all, get help. Accept treatment. Don't let shame hold you back. Screw shame. Screw labels. Screw all those who don't get it. Do whatever you have to do to get back to the real you. She's still in there. She's worth it.

Lastly, remember the positives...

You are not your diagnoses. You are not bipolar-disorder, depression, anxiety, borderline personality disorder, obsessive-compulsive disorder, posttraumatic stress disorder or any other diagnosis thrown your way. You are not your traumas. You are not anything that anyone has ever done to you. These conditions and experiences are not you. They are just a small part of you. You are so much more.

You are a warrior. You are brave. You are creative, talented, smart, and capable. You are radiant, strong, and compassionate. You are beautiful at any size. You are loved. You will get through this. It may not be today or tomorrow, but you will get through this.

Stay safe and believe. Things will get better.

Love,

Me

i'

My Journey with 'Borderline Personality Disorder'

Fiona Kennedy

T HE INVERTED COMMAS in this title are very intentional, because between the time I was diagnosed back in 2014 and the present day, I've come to a vastly different understanding of what that label means.

Let me give you a little context. I've struggled with my mental health most of my life. I was shy, anxious and introverted all through school and college. I was the epitome of the square peg in the round hole. I survived my education and emerged with reasonably good academic results, but almost no sense of self-worth.

These issues continued to plague me throughout my adult life, but until nine years ago, I could contain them enough to continue functioning. I never sought help, because it never occurred to me that I could do anything to make my life better. I simply believed that I was just a shy, awkward person who didn't fit in, and that was it.

Nine years ago, I had my first baby, and it was his arrival that precipitated my first breakdown. The second came after the birth of my daughter two years later, and by 2013, the severity and frequency of episodes had increased to such an extent that I was hospitalized for five weeks. Following this admission, and after another year of trying to get things under control with the support of my therapist and psychiatrist, I was diagnosed with borderline personality disorder (BPD).

The diagnosis terrified me, but at the same time brought huge relief because it seemed to explain the difficulties I was experiencing, in so far as my symptoms were listed as markers for the disorder. But, what scared me was everything I read about how difficult BPD is to treat. Medication and dialectical behavior therapy (DBT) seemed to be the treatments of choice. Medication I had, but the therapy I had never heard of, and I couldn't find anyone in Ireland who offered it, so I continued with my own therapist for a further year.

Throughout that time, I had periods of relative stability, but the issues would come back again and again. I was struggling with depression, with anger, with guilt. I was far too attached to my therapist and I was self-harming. Things finally came to a head in May 2015 when I overdosed on my medication. At this stage, it was agreed that I needed a more structured form of therapy than what my then therapist could provide, and so I was put on the waiting list for the only DBT program available in Galway.

The next few months proved to be long and extremely difficult. I finished with my therapist of six years, and resigned myself to waiting. I waited, and waited, and waited. My depression worsened, and within months I had been signed out of work on sick leave. Still I held on, because I knew DBT was getting closer.

Except, it never happened. At the last minute the promised program was cancelled. Mental health services in Ireland are in severe crisis, so this wasn't exactly a shock, but we were still devastated. Apart from anything else, this program was being provided by the public health service so would be free of charge. I was not in a position to pay for therapy privately, so this left us in an extremely difficult situation.

At this point I had been blogging about trying to manage my mental health for almost four years, so when I realized I was pretty much out of options, I turned to the people who had been supporting me via the blog, and set up a crowdfunding pitch. The response was unbelievable. In just twenty-four hours, I had been donated enough money to fund almost a year of therapy.

This was a massive turning point for me. Although I could no longer access DBT, I found a psychologist who specialized in compassion-focused therapy. The change that has come about in my behavior and my understanding of the whole concept of mental illness, never mind DBT, has been phenomenal. Before I started working with her, I firmly believed that BPD was something I would have to contend with for the rest of my life. I also believed I would always need to take medication, because there was a 'chemical imbalance' in my brain, that I would always need a psychiatrist and a therapist. I now know that's not the case at all.

I'm not sure I can decide where the biggest shift has been. I've realized that the label doesn't matter anymore, that I can realistically look forward to a medication free future, that BPD doesn't define me. I'm not even sure I view it as an illness anymore, because there's nothing *wrong* with my personality. I am who I am, and I've been shaped by my experiences, the society I live in, the genes I was born with—so many factors that are completely out of my control. The difficulties that I've experienced over the years aren't the result of a chemical imbalance, but a response to these factors. My most damaging behaviors came about as a means of trying to cope, of not understanding why I felt about and responded to things as I did. They kept me going for a long time, but eventually they stopped working and became a problem.

The work that I've been doing with my psychologist has taught me all of this, and so much more. She's taught me the value, even more, the necessity of compassion in order to maintain my emotional well-being. She's taught me strategies for coping with difficult emotions and situations as they arise. She's taught me that this isn't my fault, I've been doing my best all along, I just got a little lost for a while.

Mostly, she's taught me that I have a future. She's even taught me to dare to dream. I've never had that before and it's simply wonderful.

i'

·····································

Imbisoul... or
In Between Two Souls
Melissa Whelan

I DIED AT TWENTY-FIVE. In my previous life, I was a victim of rape and child molestation. Traumatic events shocked my visual memory, and I was misdiagnosed as bipolar at sixteen. I went through stages of overdose on lithium at seventeen, attempted suicide on my nineteenth birthday celebrating with twenty-eight, 150mg lithium capsules, and at twenty-three I returned to college and sought help once again due to stressful triggers. I found myself medicated on Seroquel and zombie-like and dysfunctional, I started off the semester late for class due to constant fatigue, my concentration becoming more distorted and my memory a blur. Consequently, this new behavior lead toward failure in school that I could barely understand and once the damage was done I sat in the psychiatrist's office listening to an explanation of my misdiagnosis. "We have results of the tests and analysis suggesting you have ADHD and Borderline Personality Disorder (BPD). *My Brain Needs Glasses* is a great book for ADHD and there is no medication for BPD. Psychoeducation is beneficial and we placed you on a two year waiting list."

I struggled through life afterward trying to piece together my broken life, and as I saw positive changes, I fell in love with a counsellor, and returned to my job at Videotron in the call center. Struggling for mental health resources everything else was fine until May 2016, already twenty-five years old. Lying beside my girlfriend I smelt a foul odor under the covers and days later myself felt weird bumps on my genitals. Obsessing about my health, I went to multiple hospitals to find different answers about my body. I spent the summer afraid of bugs with shivers down my spine, my immune system reacting to external factors, and I continued to obsess over my body. The people around me kept saying I was fine when I felt the opposite. I felt as though no one was listening to the point that I dissociated myself to keep in touch with reality.

Overwhelmed with the events of my life in November I was lying on a hospital table ready to remove precancerous cervical cells due to human papillomavirus (HPV). To this day I can't stop the compulsions of obsessing over my body that I cannot tell the different between somatic delusion and the reality of the situation. Writing songs is the only thing that helped bring back a glimmer of hope through dark days that threatened to encapsulate my soul.

Violated!

No violin can play away the violence

My very mind has isolated

I couldn't take it

So I tried to hide the only side

Of me I find was worth saving (saving)

I've got skeletons crushed

At the bottom of my pocket

Demons screaming in my head

don't try to stop it!

Where's my mind?

It left I lost it!

Sometimes, certain things can never be forgotten

I forgave,

And I will forgive, This,

Doesn't mean one day I won't remember what you did!

and I tried, telling myself it will be okay

it's been far too long I've been gone, in the shadows of the
day

there no tomorrow that can change the sorrows of yester-
day.

It's complicated,

Common mistakes can

Compromise comparisons of risks that I've been taking

I've been wasting my time

I haven't been fine

I can't imagine a planet where we could eliminate the lies!

My life is tragic dammit! I can't manage the damage

Stuck on a planet the language can't understand it

Well I've had it with the manic that panics

Inside of me

I want to strangle it tangle it

Till it dangles at my knees

Watch it from an angle at my ankles begging please

cuz I'm sick of you, yes you! My personality!

You let everybody trample on your feet,

you let everybody tell you what to be.

Well I didn't choose to be abused and used,

they say it's no excuse why I'm so confused.

Hand me the axe I've had enough I quit

Well fuck the past I have it doesn't mean shit!

I wrote that in May and June of 2016 to finally express my unbearable past life into the present, and without a visual in my mind I finally decided to make it so and publish it on YouTube as my artist name Imbisoul. I knew no one would have or want this name as an artist, besides the time my friend's grandmother yelled at me, "are you an imbecile?" when I took out the recycling. I told myself, *this is ridiculous, I don't deserve this!* From then on I decided "Yes I am an Imbisoul; caught in between souls!"

i

···································

Substance Abuse

"*NO ONE IS IMMUNE from addiction; it afflicts people of all ages, races, classes, and professions.*"
- Patrick J. Kennedy

i

The Past

Benjamin Tyler

I F YOU COULD GO BACK in time, what would you change in your life?

Often I am asked this very question. Upon inquiry, an inventory of memories begin flooding through my brain.

Would I erase that evening at twelve years old begging for my mother's affection, which I was denied—the point where I defined myself unlovable.

Or the dark period where I was showering with a garden hose in my dirty New Orleans apartment—a period in my life that was plagued with shame, disgusted with the man that I had become.

Maybe I should remove the time in New York City with my six-figure salary? Grinding away at soul sucking work twelve hours a day. Highlighted with frequent anxiety attacks knowing that I had a larger purpose that couldn't wait.

People always want the definitive moment—a scene that if erased, I would have never have embraced a world of drugs, alcohol, sex, porn, and gambling. And without that definitive moment or scene, I never would have relied on these vices to fill the loneliness and lack of self-worth that consumed my life.

What people forget is that they are doing exactly what that question was asking—and what I was doing for many years—they are removing my past.

Being the youngest in a household filled with backstabbing and manipulation—I saw everything. To cope, I created four rules for life:

1. Emotions will only hurt you. Shut them off.
2. Love and admiration comes from perfection. Build a life others envy.
3. Always, always stay busy.
4. When at home get to the basement as quickly as possible. The basement is where one can be alone.

Alone was safe—an internal haven where nothing could hurt me. Connection made me disconnect. Touch made me quiver. Love was nauseating. Unfortunately, "alone" never works for the soul. So, I found comfort and connection in the things that made people define me as an "addict."

At the core of my intentions was a continuous need to run. Keep relationships superficial. Always be switching cities and neighborhoods. When things got "real," I got out.

The result of always running away was a chronic need to chase something down. To fill the ego with validation for what I had become, I wanted to create a mantel-place filled with trophies for everyone to see. "Look at me! See what I built all alone! I don't need anyone!"

That was unless we were talking about the bottle. I always needed that. My Cleopatra. When she held me I could bear my soul to her. Tell her how alone I felt inside. How shameful and ugly my existence was.

Unlike my mother she always listened. Told me that I was beautiful and smart. That I would always be loved. All I had to do was keep coming back.

And coming back was exactly what I did. Every chance I could. While there was a voice inside telling me to loosen from her grips—I couldn't. Like Caesar, Cleopatra had seduced me to the point where I lost control.

The most powerful force in life is defending the person you believe yourself to be. For me, that was being a lone solder. My ego thrived on this notion. My ego. The protector from two things: not feeling worthy, and not being loved.

To break free from the ego and the vices fueling it I knew where I had to go—my story. The very thing that I was desperately avoiding. The tales I told myself and allowed to define who I was for years.

So instead of running away from the story, I decided to run into it. I got present with those past events. Relived each scene multiple times to feel the pain, regret, and shame that came with them. Had the necessary conversations with its characters. Built a community that helped me find the truth when I still wanted to listen to the lies I was telling myself.

The result was a rewritten history. A story that was more truthful, more realistic, and more uplifting. I was loved. I was beautiful. I was worthy. The story that I hated more than anything I began to love. All of its moments. All of its characters. All its pain. Who I really was and, more importantly, what I was becoming.

Through this process I was able to take control of my life. Put the power back in my hands. Life was no longer riddled with shame, but intoxicated with joy. I began walking through life not fearing who was going to hurt me, but started embracing the opportunities that come from leaning into uncertainty.

It was at that point that I could let Cleopatra go. Long before she could become the catalyst to my death. Unlike Caesar, I didn't wait too long.

And by letting her go I reclaimed life. Clarity and purpose started to fill my soul. I left that "great" job to pursue my passion of inspiring others to live bigger in their own. I left the city that attracted me for its money and women to move back to my hometown to be with family. A place I ran away from for ten years.

Snapping back to the initial question, "If you could go back in time what would you change?"

Not one thing.

i

....

Five Years Ago
Lotta Dann

I T WAS AN ORDINARY Monday afternoon. My husband would be taking our two eldest sons to their Scouts meeting shortly, and I was staying home with our baby. Outwardly there was nothing wrong with that day at all. It was a calm, ordinary Monday in our busy but functional and love-filled house. However, inside my head it was all wrong. Inside my head there was a major problem.

There was no wine in the house.

"Shall we go get some wine?" I asked my husband, trying to sound super-casual.

"Nah, let's just have an alcohol-free night." he replied. He knew I had been trying to cut back; that I had just had a heavy-drinking weekend. He heard me state that very same morning that I wasn't going to drink today.

"Ok cool," I replied, faking flippancy. I wasn't feeling flippant about it. Far from it.

Inside my head I was locked in a fierce debate. Half of me desperately didn't want to drink, so I could wake up in the morning feeling proud of myself with no guilt or hangover. The other half wanted wine so desperately it was having a major temper tantrum.

Just before 5pm my husband left the house with our two eldest boys. Now it was just me and the baby at home—and I was still locked in a fierce internal battle. I wanted this internal dialogue to stop! There was only one way out.

I plucked the baby up off the floor and actually said out loud to him, "Let's go prove how dysfunctional mum really is." I raced out of the house in such a rush that as I backed the car out of the driveway I ran over his empty pram inside the garage—I hadn't even had a drink yet!

All it took was five minutes down the road and back and I had my wine. Sweet relief as I downed the first sip.

I wasn't into savoring the taste however.

I proceeded to skull almost the entire bottle in the space of about forty minutes. I gulped down huge mouthfuls in between carrying out my housewifey duties. I changed the baby into his pajamas (gulp), the floor was vacuumed (gulp), the dishwasher loaded (gulp, gulp). I was a whirling dervish of boozy, housewifey energy.

Right before my husband was due home, I panicked. *Shit! He's going to see that I haven't managed an alcohol-free night. Shit!* In an instant I made a snap decision. *Hide the wine bottle.*

I got down on my hands and knees to reach into the back of the pantry where I tucked the nearly empty bottle of wine behind the spare boxes of tissues.

Fast forward to 3am.

I came to consciousness in my bed feeling utterly wretched. My head was pounding, my mouth dry, my guts felt sick and I had an overwhelming feeling of guilt and dysfunction.

I quietly made my way to the toilet and sat there with my head in my hands. I had been in this miserable headspace before. But this time there was a new layer of guilt. I had never hidden booze before. For the past year or so I had been desperately trying to control and moderate my long-standing enthusiastic drinking habit, yet here I was sinking even further. I could see clearly that hiding my empty bottle was a new dysfunctional drinking behavior on top of all my other dysfunctional drinking behaviors.

I felt stuck, wretched, and powerless. A huge part of me didn't want to drink that night, but yet I did. *Why the hell do I keep doing this, making promises to myself that I can't keep?* I started crying softly, there on the toilet at 3am. Miserable and at my lowest, my self-worth and self-belief shot. *I have a massive problem,* I tell myself.

Then suddenly a new thought formed in my head, and with it a glimmer of hope.

The problem isn't me. The problem is the alcohol.

I repeat it to myself.

The problem isn't me. The problem is the alcohol.

With that thought came the sense that I do have some control—and the promise of change.

The problem isn't me. The problem is the alcohol. If I take the alcohol away, the problem is gone.

And so it was, sitting there on the toilet, my cheeks wet with tears and my heart yearning for change, that I made a monumental decision.

I was going to take alcohol out of my life, and remove the substance that was causing me so much grief. I was going to solve my alcohol problem by taking the alcohol away. And I was going to learn how to live *happily* alcohol-free.

And so I did.

I have been living happily sober for five years now.

I can't even begin to describe the monumental changes I have been through since that fateful night when I hit my personal rock bottom. But suffice to say I have been through a massive process of growth and discovery.

I have learned that drinking alcohol regularly all of my adult life prevented me from developing any real emotional coping mechanisms. I have learned that I am a warm, funny, and entertaining woman without a glass of booze in my hand (and if I'm not in the mood to be social, that's okay, too). I have learned that it feels much so much better connecting with people when I'm fully present and not blurred by wine. I've learned that to be sober all the time and therefore authentic and true to myself in every type of situation is, over time, extremely calming and rewarding. And most of all I have learned that it is entirely possible to live a full, fun, stimulating, exciting and nourishing life with no alcohol in it at all.

i'

....

Depression

"THROUGH MY OWN struggles with depression, I discovered that knowledge, therapy, medication, and education can provide the strength to get through it in one place."

- Susan Polis Schutz

i'

....

Taking DeWayne
for a Run

Joshua Rivedal

HEY DUMMY. *You can't keep trying to run away from me like that. I'm always gonna be with you. No matter what. She doesn't love you. They don't love you. Shit. You don't love you. You're nothing. You're worse than nothing. You're my bitch.*

"Hey, easy. She does love me... and so do other people... I'm just tired—and sad. And I am *not* your bitch."

Yeah? Why are you here again? Sad. Miserable. Lonely—with people, lonely alone. Take a drink. Go ahead. Take twenty—no a hundred. You'll feel better.

"No. I can't. Shut the hell up. Why are you so pissed off, anyway?"

Haha. I'm not telling you. It's none of your damn business.

"I'm calling the wife... or a friend if she doesn't pick up. I don't need this right now, dude."

* * *

That's my depression talking. Needling me. Cajoling me. Laughing at me. Constantly telling me my life isn't worth living. I've been living with this character, depression, my entire life; though we only met formally six years ago after I turned twenty-seven. His name is DeWayne. He can be cool sometimes but other times he can be an arrogant d-bag. And all this extra negativity coming from him? As of the past six months or so, it's kinda my fault. I haven't been taking him on regular walks and I sure as hell haven't been taking him to the gym like I should. We do like the same music, but lately I haven't been listening to the kind he likes. And he's mad that I haven't been feeding him healthy food either. Right now, I'm holding a bottle of vodka in one hand and a glass of ice in the other but I haven't poured it yet. Sometimes I get lazy and I try to use vodka to shut DeWayne up—but recently, it's just made him louder and angrier.

* * *

Just pour the damn drink and be done with it already. When you drink, all your problems go away.

"And they come right back in the morning—we've been through this a million times."

Yeah, papi—but this time it'll be different. I promise. See? Good boy. Pour it. Put it to your lips. Good boy..."

"No," I say, slamming my drink on the kitchen counter and then pouring it down the drain. "I won't this time. I'm going outside for a smoke."

That's my boy. A cigarette. Finally, something we both can enjoy.

* * *

DeWayne is right. We both find temporary pleasure in a ciga-rette—especially since lately I haven't been taking care of him, or myself. I inhale the first drag of tar, nicotine, and pure momen-tary bliss. DeWayne is loving life right now, too. But my lungs and heart, however, are both incredibly pissed at me and have been threatening to go on strike if I don't quit smoking for good. Unlike DeWayne, both my lungs and heart have asked that their names be withheld from this story for privacy purposes.

* * *

Why are we back inside? I'm already bored. I can just keep mak-ing fun of you... or, oh I know, you can hit yourself. Remember when you used to do that?

"I haven't done that since I was thirteen. It's not going to help get us what we want—what we need."

* * *

It's tough to admit this, but from ages six to thirteen DeWayne used to tell me it was okay to slap myself in the head repeatedly when things got too intense at home or when I couldn't solve a homework problem or life problem. When I was in middle school, he had me wrap a belt around my neck after my dad got a little too physical with me. Somehow I figured out how to tell DeWayne that physically hurting myself wasn't good and I stopped. But lately he's been tempting me to start up again.

* * *

I see you looking at that bottle of sleeping pills. That would be easy. Just do it like your dad did.

"No man. We've been there before and we're not going back. It's been six years and it'll be another six hundred more."

You are such a drama queen.

* * *

I'm giving you all the bad things about DeWayne but sometimes he's good to me, too. I've had to fight so hard against him my whole life, that he's helped serve as sort of a rocket booster in the opposite direction of the feeling that I'm worthless. He can be encouraging at times, and he even lets me talk about him in public because he knows he hurts me and feels bad about it from time to time.

* * *

So you're sad, bee-yotch. So you're not getting what you want. Why even try?

"You're not my enemy. You're my friend. We've been through this before and we've made it out."

Alright... what do we do? What did we do last time?

"Well, we've got to get back into therapy—maybe you and I do couples therapy, like last time," I say going down the list of what I call my mental health first aid kit. "Get back into running. Less fried foods. Be vulnerable with the people we love. Manage expectations. And we've got to be in constant communication. If you're not feeling good, I'm not feeling good. You've got to speak up sooner and so do I. Deal?"

Fine. But less talk-y and more run-y. Come on. Get your running shoes, Mr. I'm-Gonna-Take-Action. Hurry your ass up.

"Dude. Chill. I'm putting on my running gear as fast as I can. What should we listen to while we're jogging? Coldplay?"

Dog. You know me too well. Start with "Viva la Vida." That's my jam, yo.

"Done. Let's roll," I say as we take off into the streets of Southern Los Angeles, the moon and the street lights as our only guide through side alleys, front lawns, and a thick layer of urban smog.

A LiFE OF HOPE: Discovering Me

Deeatra Kajfosz

T WAS THE 1970S AND 80S and my sense of self was a kaleido-scope of unpredictability. From being left at an abusive babysitter's home for days on end to being moved into a stranger's home for weeks with very little contact with my mother, I learned to accept my surroundings and not question. By the time we settled back into our house with some sense of pre-dictability, the rules were already being rewritten. I was an out-cast at school, my little brother an outcast at home, and my baby sister too innocent to understand it all.

Keeping secrets to hide what goes on behind closed doors was a lesson learned at a very early age. With abandonment, alcohol-ism, drug use, physical violence, verbal abuse, sexual advances, and extreme control and fear embedded within the walls of every room, it was understood that what happened within our home, stayed within our home.

By the age of twenty, I was eastward bound with husband number one at my side and expecting my eldest son. Anything to get away and make a new start. Fifteen hundred miles to separate what had been from what could be. I became a mother for the first time in early 1994. He was the love of my life and by his first birthday, we were on our own. Another marriage and baby later, and I seemed to have finally overcome my past. For all outward appearances, I had it all. Two beautiful little boys, big house on the hill, respected position in my work life, church leadership, and an engineer husband who supported adopting my little sister, moving her five states away to our Wisconsin home. Each day, I woke with the same goal; don't crack. Hide the fear. Fake it till I make it.

The spiral downward can take many shapes and the higher a person is at the time of their decent, the harder they fall. By the beginning of 2001, my grandfather had died, I had left my loveless marriage, jumped into a very unhealthy relationship, lost my independent consultant business, sold my dog to buy food, was estranged from my mother, siblings, and grandmother, and faced homelessness. As I looked into the bright eyes of my children, I was pained by how little I had to give them and how much more they deserved. I was, after all, the failure in life I had tried so very hard not to be. My head replayed every harsh reminder my mother, step-father, and childhood peers had ever spoke. I was, in fact a bastard child, ugly, stupid, weird, and nothing more than a worthless whore. The façade of confidence and value were a tattered mask. I had worn it like a stolen cloak, only to have it stripped away, one thread at a time, until the only thing left was the tattered shreds of *me*. Broken. Alone. A burden to everyone around me; most of all my children. I was the greatest hurdle they would ever have to overcome.

With a fist full of stones gripped firmly in my hands, I mentally hurled them at myself as I looked into the bathroom mirror. I reached for another bottle of pills; the name of which I couldn't pronounce. The wine was cheap and mixed with the tears that streamed down my face as I swallowed hard. I lost count of the numerous prescription and over-the-counter tablets I fed into my body. The hot water within the bathtub reflected the light of candles that broke up the darkness. As my dress submerged around me, I felt for the blade I would use to end the cycle of pain that filled my mind, heart, and pit within my gut.

No more secrets. No more shame. And no more hiding from a past I couldn't outrun. This was all I had to give. A world without me was surely the greatest gift I had to offer to those I had failed far too many times.

Sixteen years have passed since that near fateful day.

Learning to live mentally well has been a slow process but I've come a long way. I've found forgiveness to be a gift—when I've forgiven others and especially when I've forgiven myself. "Dee-atra, you can set healthy boundaries for yourself", my therapist said during a session following my survived attempt to end my life. It was then that I recognized that living is so much more than a physical journey. Having a pulse. Breathing. They serve as signs of life, but *living* is a tricky balance between logic and emotion. Growing up, I believed acceptance was entirely dependent on how well I could mirror the expectations of others. Speaking *my* truth has meant opening past pains so that they can finally be healed. I no longer treat my chronic mental illness as one that is situational. I've fought through the judgement I placed on myself to enjoy the calm that accompanies genuine trust and love. I've remarried and seen my children grow into adulthood; so many beautiful memories that never would have been. I am forever thankful for the many second chances I've been given.

I wish I could say that feelings of hopelessness are a thing of the past. But I still have days that knock me down. The defining difference is my ability to catch myself and tap into the many tools I've developed and surrounded myself with over the years. Healthy coping skills and relationships guide me through the darkness, helping me to distinguish between my fears and the hope that resides from within.

Today, I am an advocate for mental wellness and suicide prevention—serving as a public speaker and the Founder and Executive Director of a nonprofit, LiFE OF HOPE. A quote by Jon Acuff fuels my new passion for life: "Sometimes God redeems your story by surrounding you with people who need to hear your past, so it doesn't become their future." May it inspire you as well.

Life After the Ward

Imade Nibokun

THE ONLY THING I'm more afraid of than a depression melt-down is a depression lockdown. There are people who feel safe and supported when they were hospitalized, but I'm not one of them. When I was released from a secluded mental hospital that was hours away from every person who ever loved me, I thought the darkest moments of my life were over. No doctor would threaten me with drug injection or harsh medicine that made me balloon in weight. No nurse could look on me in conde-scension as if my illness deserves the punishment of a chaotic ward with yelling and physical threats lasting from the day long into the night.

When I stepped into the sun for only the second time in two weeks, I thought my trauma was over. My best friend, who flew from North Carolina and visited me every day, threw Frisbees on the immaculate lawn of my greatest nightmare to reclaim the joy that was stolen from us.

No one really tells you what life is like after the ward. You're given suicide prevention plans and a connection with a local out-patient center. But no one told me how I could hardly sleep after spending nights with antagonistic roommates and fearing sexual assault from that creepy guy who tried to enter other people's rooms.

I felt that I had just left a war, but my outpatient therapy was nothing more than a group conversation about boring topics like lawn care and cats. My mind was still thinking about the disabled crack addict who took off all her clothes to protest being stuck in a mental hospital because she was homeless. My heart was with all the people who didn't get visitors or homemade meals. You leave the ward but in many ways, the ward doesn't leave you.

To this day, I'm scared to call a crisis line because they may come to my house and take me away. I'm frightened to tell people that I'm thinking self-harming thoughts because I may lose my job. These fears aren't always based in reality. Most crisis lines don't ask for your home address. And most friends won't tell my personal issues to my boss. But that fear of going back is there. Every day of my life.

Finding therapists who don't immediately dismiss your mental healthcare trauma are hard to find. Many of them are socialized to defend their profession. Finding people who know what the inside is like, long after visiting hours, is like searching for keys in the dark. Who wants to say they were in a mental hospital when that place is used as a source of shame and comedy in popular culture?

But when you do find that therapist, and when you do find that person with shared scars, the moment is so much sweeter. The ward gives you appreciation for all the things you take for granted. The ability to see the sun, to shave, to eat what you want when you want, takes on a whole new meaning. My sense of injustice was deepened. I know the pain that is inflicted against mentally ill people. I know that despite my depression diagnosis, I lived with psychotic people and felt a small dose of the anguish they feel. My advocacy is not just for educated people with degrees, but for that crack addict, who hoped her exposed skin would lead to someone truly seeing her.

Life after the ward comes with a responsibility. You see further and deeper than most people. The ward can take away, but it can also enable you to give back.

i'

....

Finding My Sunshine
Jeanine Hoff

LOVE RAIN. I love storms even more. Clouds, thunder, sideways droplets. It calms, soothes, and inspires me to do simple things like read, paint, or bake. But we all know, it doesn't rain forever and eventually the sun comes out. Oh, the sun. Whereas the rain cleanses the soul, the sun returns to reveal it. And although I prefer gloomy weather, there is nothing more profound than the moment my life began to revolve around sunshine; internal sunshine; sunshine from my soul. I often share my journey in bits and pieces, giving the listener only what they need, but I always give them this; sunshine symbolizes the journey through a challenge, especially if that challenge is your own mind.

In the midst of the darkest days of my life struggling with anxiety and depression, I questioned what defines personal happiness and how does one master it. I always put my emotional worth into something tangible—a work project, new concept, recipe, creating a new graphic, composing a song, not just for me to see, but everyone else as well. After all, that was the only way I understood people to validate themselves. If there isn't something "to show," then how could it be real? Think about how many individuals define their validity through monetary displays: home, car, clothing, vacation. Despite this, something was terribly amiss. I began to internalize everything and focus on what happens when you appear to have it all and still lack inner self-worth—that sunshine if you will.

At the risk of sounding cliché, I thought about the song "Tomorrow" from the musical *Annie*. "The sun'll come out tomorrow," but as I waited for it, tomorrow continually felt further out of reach. I tried to "snap out of it," or "not think about it," and the more I did, the worse I felt. I realized everyone around me had the ability to just move on, while I had the ability to do the complete opposite. My "gift" was thinking about things over and over again. Going through every scenario, every possible outcome, relentlessly analyzing every word, thought, expression. Experts call this rumination. I call it self-inflicted torture.

The hardest part about this emotional tumult was that no one else seemed to understand and rightfully so. How exactly does one explain they feel awful, insignificant, useless and expect the average person to make sense of it? In my mind, everyone around me had something of value to contribute to the world and I had nothing. Even I didn't understand it. What was wrong with me? When I looked at my life on paper I knew I had a wonderful family, beautiful children, a lovely home, enjoyed great vacations, was educated and was physically healthy. On the outside, I was the embodiment of the girl who had everything. On the inside, I was a swirling tornado of unending worry, anxiety, sadness, and despair. As this mixed bag of emotions continued to eat away at my spirit, my fears began to intensify. What an uncomfortable dichotomy; feeling simultaneously worthless and fearful of practically everything.

As I continued to doubt and second-guess everything, I wrote a list of all the songs I could think of where the lyrics focused on the sun. As a musician, my knowledge of sun-themed songs was unsurprisingly vast. What I noticed was almost all shared the same idea. The sun is a constant and will eventually shine through the toughest of times. But where was my sunshine?

And like that, it appeared. I thought about what I loved to do most. Writing, graphic art, photography, educating people, rallying my community, sharing my voice and speaking on behalf of those who fear to do it themselves. Then I thought about "What am I really good at?" I'm a singer, event planner, and fundraiser. And right there is was. My sunshine. If I can create something that could help people who are at their lowest, then we can heal together.

I originally began "Where is the Sunshine?" as a means to bring people some positive inspiration. It soon evolved into something so much more. I realized this when I began tweeting my senators telling them to support mental health legislation. Within days I was blogging about things that most people keep to themselves. I knew that I could be a reasonable voice in mental health and advocate intelligently while never losing sight of those I'm trying to help. I have voiced my thoughts on mental illness and gun ownership, on mental illness, and terrorism and so much more. I knew I did not want people with mental illness to be seen as criminals, dangerous, or unreliable. I knew I wanted to educate those with mental illness, their loved ones, and the general population. I knew I wanted to speak to students, veterans, lawmakers, and corporations. In less than six months, I went from depressed to sharing positive thoughts to becoming the founder of the non-profit organization, where I work with local organizations to better support mental health.

The darkest days of my life, brought me to my brightest. My family and I have never been happier and more whole. In finding my sunshine, I found simplicity, beauty in the mundane, and the meaning of true love of family. My storm washed away my former soul and sun revealed the real me.

No Shame On U

Miriam Ament

"ONLY WANT TO talk to you when you're happy. So, let's not talk again for a while." These were the heartbreaking words I heard over the phone from one of my closest childhood friends. It didn't help that she dropped this on me during my second hospitalization for one of the deepest, darkest periods of depression that I had ever faced.

I had told very few people about my hospitalization because there was such a stigma, like I was "less than," and I already felt so alone and isolated. But having a close childhood friend make feel like a pariah just for having a brain disorder—it took my misplaced shame and loneliness to a whole new level. She would never have said those words to me if I was in the hospital because my leg was broken or needed heart surgery. Needless to say, my hospital stay was significantly extended, in no small part because of that close childhood "friend"—who I never heard from again.

{ 155 }

Both my first and second hospitalizations occurred when I was thirty and thirty-one years old. I was living in New York City at the time, a home away from home where I had gone to both undergraduate and graduate school. After my second hospitalization, I decided to start fresh and move to LA—I love entertainment and pop culture and was excited at the prospect of working in casting for TV and film. I soon found that even though I was in a new place with countless opportunities, without the right support and treatment, I was not going to get any better. Within a year, I was back in Chicago living in my parents' house and ended up being hospitalized once again.

I decided I couldn't live like this anymore and sought out the right therapist and psychiatrist to get on the road to recovery, which I now took very seriously. I worked on my mental health almost religiously. I never missed a therapy session and always made sure to take my medication. Soon, I took a job in a law firm and was able to move out of my parents' house and live on my own again. I started dating a man who would soon become my husband.

But I still wasn't completely free—the chains of stigma wouldn't loosen their grip on me. I felt like I had to keep my mental health condition a huge secret from anyone who wasn't my husband or who didn't know me at the time of my hospitalizations.

Fast forward to almost a decade after meeting my husband, I won a charity auction and had the opportunity to go to lunch with the legendary actress Glenn Close. I knew that she was a huge mental health advocate and I felt safe enough with her to tell her my entire story—the first person other than my husband who I was completely open with. She was incredibly receptive and affected by my story in a positive way. I thought if I can tell Glenn Close my story, I can tell anyone—and maybe prevent them from all the pain I suffered because of stigma.

So, I sought out a fellowship for social entrepreneurs, at the time called JCC PresenTense, and created an organization, No Shame On U. Little by little, I began to tell people my story but didn't do anything in a big way until October of 2014 when I did a segment on the local news for National Depression Screening Day. That lead to a cover story about No Shame On U in a local Chicago publication. The reception I received from people after sharing my story was better than anything I could ever have imagined. It resonated with so many people to the point that people were writing me saying that because of me, they were able to seek help after weeks, months, and even decades of silence due to stigma.

Most importantly, the response showed that our community was really in need of an organization like No Shame On U, which is dedicated to eliminating the stigma associated with mental health conditions.

Soon enough, community members and volunteers were rallying around our efforts, helping us with community outreach programs, educational presentations on mental health and stigma, the creation of online tools and resources for mental health and so much more.

Research shows that stigma is one of the key barriers to people seeking mental health treatment. It also shows that one of the best ways to break the stigma is for people to have contact with individuals living with a mental health condition—real, kind, compassionate people; people like me. After keeping it a secret for ten years, I tell my story wherever they'll let me through the door: synagogues, community mental health nights, speaker meetings, and forums—all in an effort to be part of the change to break stigma once and for all.

After hearing my story, this is an email I received from a family member of a person living with a mental health condition:

"Hi Miriam, our family was so touched by your presentation and inspired by all of your efforts. Today was an important day for us. Because of you, we are comfortable moving forward to educate ourselves and become involved. Thank you."

If I had to go through everything I went through—the pain, the terrible stigma—all to help this one family, then it was all worth it.

Bipolar Disorder

....

"*MY RECOVERY FROM* manic depression has been an evolution, not a sudden miracle."

– Patty Duke

There Comes a Light

Elaina J. Martin

IPOLAR DISORDER. Those words never meant much to me until I experienced my first unexplained mixed episode. I had just moved to California to be a Style Editor for an up-and-coming website. I adored my title: 'Style Editor.' I had worked so hard in New York and Texas to finally land a gig I had always wanted on the West Coast.

But Style Editors don't try to overdose and kill themselves, which is exactly what I did. I took enough Xanax to warrant a 911 call from my new roommate. An ambulance. The ICU. Parents flying in from Oklahoma. I nearly died and I didn't know why.

In the psych ward I was in some kind of mental stupor. I believe it was the number and dosages of the drugs that didn't allow me to articulate most of my vocabulary; that made me forget everything. Then again, it could have been mania.

{ 161 }

Calls came in to the hospital from around the country - friends and family wishing me well. Flowers arrived from my new bosses. My parents and sister brought me a bouquet of roses in my favorite shade of blush pink which we had to put in a plastic cup on the floor by my bed because I couldn't be trusted with glass. My sister's best friend made me brownies. It was as though everyone was trying to say, "Stay. We love you. Don't ever go," but what I also thought I heard in their voices was, "Why, Elaina?"

After seventy-two hours in the psych ward, I flew back to Oklahoma to live with my parents. This was a harrowing time. I had been living on my own for a decade and then, there I was at twenty-seven, needing to live with my parents. I had to resign from a job I had always wanted with a salary to match. Though plagued by depression for years, this was a new kind of depression. One of which every ounce of my energy was zapped. The love seat in the living room became my world.

It took a long time to get out of that dark depression that came on that fall and lasted through the winter of 2008 and 2009. I had been blogging for years and by the summer of 2009 I had my own website. I wrote about what it felt like to be sick, but never wrote the words 'bipolar disorder' or 'mental illness.' I was scared of losing friends who didn't know about my diagnosis. That had already happened. Some of my old friends just didn't know how to handle me and my ever-changing moods. I think some were ignorant and, thus, scared and I didn't really blame them. Before my diagnosis I knew nothing about bipolar disorder.

But hiding secrets is exhausting. It starts to eat at your insides. I felt so much shame. I felt like somehow I was less than who I had been before I was sick. I was tired – of lying, of hiding, of feeling that awful shame. So, I came out of the 'bipolar closet' in a blog I titled, "Be Brave, Elaina J." I couldn't sleep the night I posted it. I worried who I would lose and I had already lost so much, but the next day I was overwhelmed by the love and compassion I was shown from my friends, family, and readers.

Coming out of the 'bipolar closet' was one of the best things I have ever done. By learning to live a life of authenticity I could share what it meant to be sick, but also what it meant to be well.

I began writing and completed my memoir, *There Comes a Light: A Memoir of Mental Illness.* I started writing the very popular blog "Being Beautifully Bipolar" on the Psych Central website. Because I was navigating the illness and the medication management and creating support systems, all while experiencing episodes of depression, mania, and mixed episodes; I could help others find their own way through the chaos that is mental illness. All I wanted to do was to help people feel less alone in their own struggles. I wanted to use my writing to let people know that there was someone else out there who understood and wanted to help them.

I have become known as a mental health advocate. People and nonprofits seek me out as an expert on bipolar disorder, and I guess I am. I live it every hour of every day for at least the past eight years. I know how dark depression is. I know how high mania can take you. I know about impulsivity and lethargy. I get it and if I can help people to get through that darkness—to know that there is still light or talk them off the roof, as it were, during mania, well, then I have done my job.

Ten Years After Diagnosis

Cynthia Forget

T'S HERE! SEPTEMBER 25, 2015. That's ten years from the day I was first diagnosed with bipolar disorder. It's hard to believe it's been that long, and yet in some ways it seems like a lifetime ago. And it really was. It was a different life before I got sick. Bipolar disorder has no "cure." It is a chronic, progressive illness that will forever be a part of my makeup.

Trouble is, bipolar disorder has stolen so many of my memories. It's hard to visualize my life before my illness. It has taken over that much. I remember big picture things rather than details. For example, I know we were a happy family—my husband and two children. We did a lot of typical family stuff. We did them together. That means I actually participated in activities and outings. Once I was sick that didn't happen often.

When I was diagnosed my children were only 11 and 6. My illness made a huge impact on my family, my marriage, my career and my life. When I was manic I wasn't around much. I was out being busy—shopping, partying, working on projects or anything else that was an energy release. Unfortunately, little of that energy was spent at home.

When I was home, it was usually because I was depressed. And if I was depressed, I was in bed. And I stayed there. Not moving for days, weeks, even months on end. My children became used to seeing me in that state. To them I was just sad. And it was sad. I missed out on so much—so did they.

But through it all, somehow I managed to instill in them my values, and I was able to be there for them emotionally. Though I was no longer able to do all the typical mothering type things that I was used to doing, like volunteering at school, driving them to friends' houses, helping with homework., I did what I believe to be even more important. I nurtured them. I groomed them for life. I taught them unconditional love.

Before bipolar I actually had a life. I had friends—most of them deserted me. I had a career—my behaviour was off the wall. I escaped with emotional bruises and ended up on long-term disability. I was a fun person to be around—I think I was happy. I was a companion to my husband in every way. We went out often. We talked a lot. We laughed a lot. We were very much a couple and had an active social life. That all changed. In addition to bipolar disorder, I struggle with general anxiety and social anxiety. That keeps me away from most things and most people.

In the time that has passed I've learned a lot about bipolar disorder. I have researched the subject beyond what you could imagine. I have applied much of what I have learned. And as the time has passed I have discovered better ways of coping and better ways of predicting and even preventing future episodes. I've had to adjust my lifestyle considerably. My life is now a fragment of what it used to be. But I'm okay with that. Most days.

In the ten years that have passed, I've tried countless medications and even more combinations and doses. I'm probably in the best place I've been since this all started. I call this "recovery." Recovery is different for everyone. It happened for me when all the necessary elements came together: I was finally prescribed the right medication cocktail; was receiving worthwhile therapy and psychiatric care; made the necessary lifestyle changes; and had a successful support network. This is my tool kit. And when all these factors align, I feel I'm in recovery. Recovery is not one thing, but rather a process of stages. Generally, it's a slow road.

But this illness does not rest and it does not stay the same. It changes with brain chemistry. It changes with situations. Even though my days are mostly good right now, I remain on guard knowing that my mood can fluctuate at a moment's notice. I often ruminate over my losses – friends, career, cognitive function and lifestyle.

I live in fear of relapse. The course of bipolar disorder dictates that I will. What would relapse look like? Would I find myself back in bed, hiding from the world? Or will I embark on a damaging manic episode? What will happen to my life? Will the people who have been standing by me stay? Or will it be too much for them to handle, again? How will I cope? That's a lot of questions. And I'm afraid of the answers.

Though this is not the life I signed up for, I'm not bitter. I don't hate that I have bipolar disorder. It's a part of me now. It has taught me a lot. And it has given me strength. There are many ways I can still find happiness. Today will be today. I can't change that. I've learned that and I accept that. That is an important lesson. My goal now is to lead a productive, meaningful life with as few bipolar interruptions as possible. But still, any way you slice it, I'm not the same person I was ten years ago. I miss my old life. I miss me.

i'

·····································

Laura: Version 2.0
Laura Marchildon

FOR MOST OF MY LIFE I've been a teacher. In my first career, I taught children and youth with autism and developmental delays. My next career I switched to the fire service where I taught groups of all ages about fire and life safety. I held that position until I was forty-one, when one day I stopped being able to teach, or even function as the "normal" me; a loving fiancée and mother to two tween girls.

I still shudder at how surreal that day's events seem. I put on my fire uniform, tied my tie, drove to work, chatted with my coworkers, and then proceeded with what was a typical day on the job. While at an industrial site with some fire fighters, I suddenly stopped walking and was completely unresponsive. My coworkers brought me home where I perked up a bit and found the energy to cook steaks. Later in the day, I was outside with my husband watching him work. At some point I went into the house, took a knife and cut my forearm five times. After, I found my husband and said, "honey I've been a bad girl." He immediately took me to the hospital where I apparently agreed to be admitted. I didn't wake up from this nightmare until five days later.

Upon returning home, I was an emotional wreck with rapid changing and unpleasant feelings that I had never experienced. My brain felt broken. I couldn't read. I couldn't write. And I had to resort to doing children's word search puzzles. It became incredibly confusing to try to process what people were saying when they talked to me, and my ability to multitask was shot. Worst of all, I felt spiritually disconnected. I no longer knew who I was and what my purpose was in the grand scheme of life.

I soon began to see a psychiatrist who diagnosed me with Bipolar II—which made perfect sense... and no sense at all. How could I, at 41, have Bipolar II when the typical age of onset is 18-25? On the other hand, mental Illnesses run rampant on my paternal side of the family. But then again I had no previous symptoms. I should have free and clear. I had to accept my diagnosis and find some way to move forward. It wouldn't be easy.

After multiple drug treatments my psychiatrist and I decided that I would try Electroconvulsive Therapy. Unfortunately, after several sessions it did not alleviate my depression and negatively impacted my memory, so we decided I would have to try another course of treatment.

I was then referred to a counselor who practiced Dialectal Behaviour Therapy (DBT). I worked hard during my sessions, and I gave my homework my all but it just wasn't working out. Irrational thoughts due to my "broken brain" still had a hold on me.

It wasn't until the following year, when I took Cognitive Behaviour Therapy (CBT) that I began to learn some valuable tools that helped me cope and manage my bipolar—skills that have helped me even to this day. During one of my initial CBT sessions, my counsellor saw me struggling and pulled me aside. "I'm just... frustrated at everything I used to be able to do that I can't do anymore," I said fighting back tears.

"In order for you for you to begin the healing process, you have to grieve for the loss of the old Laura," the counsellor replied.

This was my "a-ha" moment—the cartoon light bulb over my head! The counsellor was absolutely right! The old Laura was dead and gone. Why was I wasting time trying to be like her? Once I accepted that, I could start working on a new me.

In addition to being a teacher, I have always been a lifelong learner. Since my "a-ha" moment, I've done countless hours of research on Bipolar Disorder. I've read memoirs, autobiographies, Bipolar Disorder workbooks, Bipolar Disorder self-help books, books about the Bipolar brain, articles on brain exercises, blogs on mindfulness, and journal papers on CBT and DBT. The more I could learn about my mental illness, the more control I could have over it—because knowledge is power.

Currently my day-to-day presents tremendous challenges and I have to push myself to do everything. Reading and writing are still difficult but I can actually do both (sometimes using an old paperback dictionary and thesaurus)! I can't multitask any longer and I require lists to keep my life in order—and that is all ok. I've improved so much over the last seven years—so much so that in March 2016, I decided to share my story on a bigger scale in the hopes that it would help others with mental illness or their loved ones.

I created a website and blog and I set up accounts on other social media platforms. It's incredible how many people will message me on Facebook or Twitter just so they can have someone listen to them. The material I posted on my blog was a mix of education, pictures, and even my grayer days when my depression would flare up. Soon enough, I found that my posts were resonating with people and they began asking me for more articles, more advice, and more educational content. And it was then that I realised that not all of the old Laura was gone after all. With my blog, I was tapping into Laura the teacher and educator.

Yes, I have had to accept that my Bipolar Disorder is simply a part of me now. "It is what it is," as the saying goes. But I have been able to reboot myself and my life to Laura: Version 2.0 (batteries not included)—and that, no one can ever take away from me.

White Lines
Kate Dolan

I HAVE THE WORD "BREATHE" tattooed on my left wrist. It's my little reminder to breathe when I feel anxious, overwhelmed, or upset. For several years I got really nervous whenever someone asked to see it. It wasn't because the tattoo was botched or misspelled—the tattoo itself is flawless. It's what below it that made me feel ashamed and embarrassed: five white lines across my wrist. A constant reminder of that night I almost lost the battle against my mental illness.

I always knew something about me was different. I cried easily as a child and was quick to get upset when things would suddenly change, which made it difficult for me to connect with other kids. My parents would say, "Kate's just very sensitive," but I always wondered why my emotions seemed so much more intense than others.

I was thirteen the first time I cut myself. After being teased yet again for being "over sensitive" I took out my aggression on myself. My mom discovered what I was doing and brought me to my first therapist. At fourteen I saw my first psychiatrist and began the long and painful road of life with a mental illness. I was diagnosed with depression, then anxiety, and finally bipolar disorder type II.

For eight years I saw more psychiatrists, psychologists, social workers, and other mental health workers than I can count. I've been hospitalized and treated with ten different medications and various combinations. But it wasn't the hurt of doctors who didn't get me, the frustration of trips to the hospital to get my lithium levels checked, or even the side effects of the different meds that bothered me—it was how ashamed I felt of my mental illness that made it intolerable.

I used to pray every night to a God I didn't even believe in to make my pain stop. All I wanted was to be normal and happy. People were afraid of me when they found out about my mental illness, and it broke my heart because it wasn't something I could control; it was something I was afraid of myself. I tried to hide my medication and the books my parents bought me about bipolar disorder. I lied about where I was going when I went to therapy or to get my lithium levels checked. I left the classroom, party, or any situation when I felt like my moods were becoming unstable and said I just didn't feel well. The more I tried to hide my mental illness from the world, the more I realized I was hiding it from myself and the worse it got. I drank to make the feelings stop which only led to mania and mistake after mistake. I couldn't accept that I had a mental illness because I had learned from society that it wasn't ok to have one. But I'm learning that that's not true. There's nothing wrong with having a mental illness and getting the treatment that you need.

My favorite psychologist always told me not to say that I am bipolar, instead I should say I *have* bipolar disorder. Bipolar disorder does not define me; it's just something that I live with. I finally decided I wasn't going to let it rule my life so I learned how to treat it. Once I got on the right meds and started taking better care of myself with diet, exercise, sleep, and meditation, I realized that living with bipolar disorder didn't have to be so hard. I also realized that having a mental illness doesn't make me or anyone else living with one weird, scary, or crazy. Living with bipolar disorder has made me incredibly strong and resilient as well as compassionate towards others, which are things I love about myself. I don't feel this way every day but I do my best to acknowledge and accept my mental illness because when I don't it starts to get the best of me. There are days when I can come to terms with it and there are other days I cry hysterically in the bathroom begging for this to go away. But I've noticed that when I take care of myself and try to accept the hand I was dealt, it gets easier. I can't do it alone though, so I'm building a team of loved ones, my psychiatrist, my therapist, and a bipolar support group. This is a lifelong battle and I've armed myself to fight it.

I don't hide my scars anymore because I've come to accept them as a part of me. Just like my bipolar disorder, they don't define me. If people see them and feel uncomfortable around me then that's their problem, not mine. I'm open about my mental illness and write about it to educate others and help those who also suffer know they're not alone. It's also another form of therapy for me. I don't look at my scars as a reminder that I was weak; I look at them as a badge of honor. They remind me that I am resilient and that I can overcome all the struggles that come with my mental illness. I've decided never to cover them up because I'm not ashamed anymore—I have nothing to hide.

Postpartum Depression

"*THE VERY DAMAGING, frightening part of postpartum is the lack of perspective and the lack of priority and understanding what is really important.*"

– Brooke Shields

Post-Parting Depression

Suzi Leigh

I WAS PREPARED. Beyond preparation, I had envisioned myself as a mother so many times that I had nearly begun believing that I lived those moments. Holding my baby as if I had done it a million times, nursing him with a natural ease, and gently, yet effectively laying him down to sleep after a day of baby-wearing all seemed so real that up until I entered the doors of the hospital believed that I knew what I was doing.

As I made those final urgent and panicked pushes, my baby made his way earth-side and I felt immense pride. "I did it," I tearfully said to my husband, as the weight of the last nine months trickled from my body and out into the room. But something happened then; our baby didn't cry the way they do in the movies and the birth videos I had so studiously watched. He didn't make any

{ 179 }

sound at all. The nurses took him over to the table to check him and my husband followed, leaving me alone hooked up to a machine. Within moments, he cried, but his breathing was shallow, and so he was monitored for the next hour before his lungs were suctioned out. It turns out he had inhaled meconium, which is sticky like tar.

In my breastfeeding class we learned about the importance of the first hour of birth to establish a healthy latch. It was imperative to connect baby to breast and get colostrum into baby's body. As I watched the nurses gather around my baby all I could do was sit with the reality that my planning was already failing. I didn't get him on my chest, I didn't get to breastfeed him, and I was already not the mother I wanted to be.

For the first six months after my first son's birth, I sank in guilt and let it swallow me whole. Every nursing session, every time he cried uncontrollably for over an hour, every night as I tried to lay him down with no success, I blamed myself. I had prepared for what kind of mother I was going to be, but all of my attempts to find her left me deflated.

During the first three months postpartum, I didn't know many other mothers, especially ones around my age. I knew I should have gone out and tried to socialize, but it took me finally going to see a doctor to pull me out of isolation. Her recommendation was to join a playgroup, go to the breastfeeding support group at the hospital, and go on a low dose antidepressant. The last part was a suggestion and she made it clear it was up to me. I was no stranger to antidepressants and had no issues taking medication, especially since I wanted to ensure that I had every tool necessary to take care of my baby and myself.

I never let myself feel guilty for taking medication, because I knew that the best possible way to take care of my family was to first and foremost take care of myself. If I let myself sink deeper and deeper into my depression, it would cause a ripple effect that would harm my family, and the last thing I wanted to do was hurt the ones I loved. But most important, I needed to sit with myself and realize that I alone was reason enough to get better. If you took away my entire family, wouldn't I still be worth working on?

Unsurprisingly, the part that made the biggest difference in my mental state was meeting other mothers. Getting out of the house and our daily routine and talking to women who were facing the same difficulties made me realize that there is a difference between failing and struggling—and that I was not alone. Everything I was feeling was a part of the life altering experience I had just gone through.

I was struggling hard, but I was not failing, because I had not given up. I was trying, every single day, to become a better mother. I didn't like crying as much as I was and I didn't enjoy comparing myself to the mother I had envisioned for myself. But a few months into my recovery, I finally realized that what happened during my son's birth was in no way my fault, that birth is an unpredictable process, and preparation does not always equal success. I developed a hope that things would someday get better, that one day I would look back on this time and see how far I'd come and how much I learned from that experience. I wished for the day that I would stop having such high expectations for myself and maybe even let some things roll off me without reacting emotionally; and that one day I might be able to tell a struggling new mother that I understood, because I was there once, and I made it through. I'm proud to say I did, and so can you.

Riding the Wave of Postpartum Depression

JoAnne Diaz

HAD EXPERIENCED Postpartum Depression once before so I knew what to do to *try* and prevent it from rearing its ugly head again in my life. I was able to avoid it for a few years and then maybe without recognizing it or intending to—I got *cocky*. I became lax and then, out of nowhere not only was it there staring at me in the face but it was unlike something I had ever endured before.

I had just had my ninth child. A week later I moved into a new home. I was sleep deprived but I continued to go through the motions because I had no choice but to unpack us all and keep on forging ahead like us moms always do. It didn't matter though because Postpartum Depression hit me so bad and so fast that it literally knocked me to the ground. My mind began racing, I could not sleep even if I wanted to, the anxiety set in, the panic attack hit and I had my husband call for an ambulance. I thought I was going to die then and there.

With the help of the medical community, my family, my friends and my church community I was able to slowly creep out of the rut of Postpartum Depression and anxiety. It was not easy by any means and it was not quick. There were many days I did not want to be alone for fear—fear of dying and fear of killing myself or killing my children. For a while I was not able to do that which was so normal for me to do every day all day long. I watched as other people cleaned my house, made us meals and the like. I watched as my husband took care of my children and even the newborn baby. It was as if I was not living in my body. I was a prisoner who didn't even have enough energy to want to be set free. I was plagued with anxiety which is something I had never experienced before. Panic attacks would occur sometimes without any trigger or warning what-so-ever. There were days that I felt that I was making progress and then there were days where I felt like I was back to the beginning.

One thing that I knew very early on was that when I survived this bout of Postpartum Depression I would do something to help other women experiencing it. While riding the ups and downs of this illness, I would take time to make notes on what I was experiencing so I would not forget the intensity of it all. When the time came and though still not even close to feeling 100% better, I began writing a book on Postpartum Depression. I was so passionate about expressing the severity of the illness that, similar to the famous movie character *Forest Gump,* I basically wrote the book almost all in one sitting. Once the book was published I got involved in reaching out to the medical community and postpartum forums to share my experience. I was on a mission to break the stigma about Postpartum Depression and to give a voice, a bullhorn, to something that so many women experience on a daily basis but that some don't survive.

There is something about not having control over an illness you can do nothing about yet wanting to take a bad experience and give it purpose. I did not want anyone else to experience what I did. I did not want family members and friends to have to witness a loved one go through what I did and not know what to do or how to help. I wanted women to know that they can survive Postpartum Depression and live not only a happy life with their child but they can thrive. I did not want women to feel defined by their illness. One can experience something but it does not have to define them.

I would not wish Postpartum Depression on my worst enemy. Yet, I learned a lot from it and, having come out on top of it I can honestly say that I am actually thankful for having had it. I learned to appreciate people more. I had a new found respect and deep sympathy for any person experiencing any type of mental illness. I discovered a whole new way to enjoy my life, my husband and my children; to literally stop and smell the flowers because one never knows if he will lose his sense of smell at any moment or even, if the flowers won't be there at all.

Postpartum Depression was and still is a wave for me. It is something I may struggle with for the rest of my life. Only time will tell. But like anyone in any given body of water: you either sink or swim. I chose to keep swimming because even though I could not see it I knew there was a shore.

Kicking Postpartum's Ass

Jen Schwartz

O N MARCH 25, 2013, a very pregnant woman goes into labor during the first night of Passover dinner in front of thirty of her closest Jewish family members. She has one hand under the table death gripping her sister's and the other on her iPhone timing her contractions while simultaneously texting her mom-friends who have already done this labor thing.

After one friend tells her to "call the effing doctor" because the contractions are so irregular and close together, she listens. With the hospital bag already packed and in the car, her husband drives her to the hospital as she thinks to herself, *At least I don't have to sit through the endless post-meal portion of the Seder.*

She immediately requests the epidural because she has no interest in feeling all the painful feels that come with the miracle of childbirth. After twenty-four hours of labor, pushing for two, and having a C-section anyway, she finally welcomes the baby boy she's waited nine months to meet. Although feeling quite stoned from all the medications, she's moved to the room she will call home for the next three days and is greeted by the crew of new Jewish grandparents, great grandparents, aunts, and uncles all wanting to meet Mason Luke Schwartz, the baby boy they have also waited nine months for.

Her hospital stay is unremarkable. She always has visitors. She overdoses on turkey and brie sandwiches. She tries to rest. She attempts to breastfeed her son and supplements with formula. When it's time to go home she fills out a survey and checks all the boxes that imply the highest levels of happy-new-mom.

On the second day home from the hospital, something seems wrong. She seems distanced and sad. She never wants to get out of bed. She makes excuses for why she has no interest in that adorable baby boy in the next room. Her light has gone out and is replaced by something else.

* * *

That mom is me and that something else that stole the beginning months of motherhood from me is postpartum depression. An illness I never believed could happen to me. An Illness I had no idea affected 1 in 7 new moms each year. An illness that convinced me I had made a terrible mistake deciding to become a mother.

I could tell you about how I knew something was wrong when I constantly thought about getting sick or injured so I could go back to the hospital where I wouldn't have to take care of my baby. Or how I woke up every morning at 6 a.m. with paralyzing anxiety and could barely breathe. Or how I would walk circles around my neighborhood trying to calm the anxiety while ugly crying on the phone to my mom that I would never get better. Or how I barely left the house for five months and spent much of that time medicated and in bed. Or how I couldn't understand why everyone else fell in love with and rocked this whole motherhood thing, while I failed miserably at it. Or how I thought my therapist was lying to me every week when she promised me I wouldn't feel like this forever. And on top of feeling this awful, also feeling overwhelmingly guilty for sleeping through almost the first six months of my son's life.

But... let's talk about what happened when I got better instead. When I made the choice to accept my diagnosis, ask for help, and follow through with the right treatment for me, which was weekly therapy sessions with a psychologist who specialized in postpartum mood disorders (who I still see) and medication (that I still take) under the care of a psychiatrist.

I can still remember the first solo walk Mason and I took to the park. The first date night I had with my husband. The first photo where I smiled and wasn't faking it. And most importantly, the discovery of a tremendous inner strength and incredibly loud voice that I didn't know I possessed.

When I began to write about my experience, I heard from so many moms who I knew and strangers who struggled like I did. I wondered why people didn't talk more about postpartum depression and the risk factors. Maybe if I was more aware and more educated, I could have been more proactive. I would have known what was happening to me right away, that I was not alone, and there were resources and people out there to help me get better.

I decided that I would use my newfound strength and voice to be the person who always talked about postpartum depression by sharing my story, educating others, and bringing awareness to this mental illness that affects so many moms each year. That courage and honesty are contagious, and together, we can destroy the stigma and make life easier for those who come after us.

If you have postpartum depression, you're in good company—the company of hundreds of thousands of women—many of whom fought the stigma and shame that surrounds postpartum depression just like I did, but also too many who don't even realize they have a common, treatable illness. Women who don't speak out because they are too ashamed or afraid someone will take their babies away. Women who don't know where to go for help. Women who end up suffering in silence because they don't realize they don't have to.

It's these women who I will always speak up for. Who I'm committed to destroying the stigma for. My illness doesn't define me. I am not ashamed. I didn't ask to get sick. I didn't do anything wrong. I'm not a failure or a horrible mother because it took me longer to bond with my baby and embrace the joys of motherhood. I define who I am. I am the author of my story. And you are too.

Eating Disorders

"*EATING DISORDERS ARE serious mental illness, not lifestyle choices.*"

– Demi Lovato

The Eating Anorexia
Heather Williams

AS LONG AS I CAN RECALL, I have had a complicated relationship with food. I love food. I was raised in the South where all events, big or small, happy or sad, revolve around food. We Southerners use food as a way to show love or appreciation for someone. Your aunt is sick? Let me bring you a casserole. You just got a promotion? Let me make you a celebratory supper. You're coming over to visit on a Tuesday? Let me make you something delicious, honey! I also hate food, or more accurately, hate what food can do to me. Food can control me, make me angry, make me doubt myself, and skew the way that I view myself. Food and I are in a co-dependent relationship. He makes me feel bad but I just can't let him go.

It wasn't until several years ago I realized that the way that I viewed food and myself differently than other people. I assumed everyone, especially women, thought like I did. When people would make comments about my size and it seemed weird to me; I compared it to people complementing a less than attractive baby. People always say how cute the baby is because they are *supposed* to say that the baby is cute. Nobody ever says the baby is ugly! That's kinda how I think: people would say I was small because they were being polite, not because it was real. One day, a coworker told me that she thought I had an eating disorder. What? No. That's ridiculous. Wait? Was it?

That conversation was a sort of Aha moment for me. I had never entertained the idea that I have an eating disorder. After that statement, I started thinking of all my thoughts and behaviors around food. Restricting my food? Check. "Good" foods vs "bad" foods? Check. Extreme guilt after eating? Check. Lying about how much I ate? Check. Have a funhouse mirror view of my body? Check. I tried sharing some of this with friends but I was often met with statements about how I was "searching for compliments" or "oh... yeah. I wish I had your skinny girl problems." I wasn't. I was searching for some validation that what I was thinking mattered. So, I stopped talking.

Fast forward to a couple years ago. I was talking to a friend and we were sharing some of our personal struggles. I felt comfortable enough with him to share some of my daily thoughts and feelings around food, eating, and how I view my body. "So you are an eating anorexic." What? No. Wait. Maybe? That statement made sense. I was validated. I felt as if what I thought, and felt, and believed about myself mattered. I was able to have a name (albeit an odd one) to what I was experiencing. Slowly over the next year, I shared a little more about my struggles to other people, but only my husband and close friends. Although it was difficult for me to verbalize exactly what I experience, I was met with acceptance and an attempt to understand. They supported me, asked questions, and most importantly, treated me the same as they did before they knew my secret.

Last year, a close friend asked me to present on an Eating Disorders Recovery Panel. What? No. Why me? I was terrified of presenting on that panel because I thought that I wasn't "sick enough". I am not diagnosed with an eating disorder. You can't count all my ribs. I eat. I don't look like the stock photos of anorexia we are shown. I felt like I would be a fraud. I believed that I wasn't "sick enough" because I believed every one of the stereotypes of an eating disorder. So, he set up a meeting for me to meet with one of the other panelists. Over coffee, I shared my concerns of not being diagnosed with an eating disorder while also sharing some of my thoughts and beliefs about food, my body, and the feelings of guilt I experience after eating. As she nodded at every one of the statements, I felt validated. I sat on the panel and for the first time shared openly my daily struggles with an eating disorder. Nobody cared that I wasn't diagnosed with an eating disorder; the thoughts, feelings, beliefs, and pain were the same as those that have been diagnosed.

Finally, I was free after years of being in denial; yes, I still have it, but now I feel more in control of it. In fact, I see it as a strength instead of a debilitating weakness. My eating disorder has given me an ability to empathize with others on a level that I may have not been able to without it. I can understand how irrational beliefs and thoughts can run your life and how exhausting that can be. I know that this is a daily, sometimes minute by minute, struggle. I know how fear of being judged and stereotypes about mental illness can hinder people from openly talking about their struggles or seeking help. I have experienced the feeling of being misunderstood, dismissed, and "attention seeking". More importantly, I have experienced how validation, support, and an attempt of understanding can result in recovery.

I learned that all the other parts of me were not going to be overshadowed by the label and stereotype of an eating disorder. My realization of this has led me to help others with a mental illness realize that it is only a part of them-not all of who they are. My eating disorder doesn't *define* me, it's only *one* part of me. By the way, Food and I still have a complicated relationship but we talked about it and I think it's going to work out ok.

i'

....

Enough

Molly Hillery

I SAT IN MY PSYCHIATRIST'S office, staring angrily out the window. I pulled my knees to my chest and sighed heavily, hoping my shift in body language would send him the message that I wasn't interested.

This scene was not new to me. I was enduring my second round of intensive treatment for anorexia and after relapsing, was once again living nearly 800 miles away from home. A month into it this time, I was pulled into my attending psychiatrist's office for what they called "non-compliance." Basically, I was struggling to complete meals, among other concerning behaviors. I was also eloping, self-harming often, and had already spent a weekend in the hospital for acute suicidality. A large part of this was due to the fact that I was finally feeling things I had avoided for years. I was also desperately trying to find a productive combination of medications, and was working on restoring physical health as well. I felt like an utter mess, and it was starting to affect the way my treatment team approached me.

My psychiatrist was not as accommodating and understanding as he usually was. He was tired of my behavior- I could tell. I met his frustration with rebellion and a stubborn attitude.

Encounter Report: December 16, 2013

I met with Molly. She was tearful earlier and said it was related to not feeling well physically, and has been struggling with weight acceptance, as she feels she has reached her target weight, or is close. This translated into difficulties with meal plan completion. She refused afternoon snack and had hidden part of her lunch. She did not make this up. She denies any other compensatory behaviors, but continues to have high urges to restrict her food intake.

When asked to explain my behavior, I firmly stated, "I've just had enough."

The follow-up question was obvious. Enough of what? I came up with a million reasons why I was done with treatment, and another thousand excuses for why I deserved a break from recovery (and a day of skipping meals). "I'm tired of working hard, I'm not feeling well, I need some space, therapy is too difficult, I miss home, my meds don't feel right." And while these things all felt very true in my mind, he was not buying what I was selling. I was hoping this would persuade him to give in and let me go on my (un)merry way, but it failed.

What I expected after my speech was disapproval, a long lecture, and the threat of discharge. Instead, he responded with this firm, but resolute response:

"You have had enough? Let me explain something to you: Your eating disorder is like an abusive partner. It tells you all of these things that aren't true, yet you stay so attached to it. You keep coming back for more and giving in to its demands. Saying 'I've had enough' shouldn't be used as an excuse to give up. Picture this: An abused wife is beaten round the clock by her husband- this last beating was particularly bad. She doesn't know what is different this time, but she knows she needs to get out. For her, but also for her children. She rounds up the kids in the middle of the night, gets in her car, and finally takes off, for good. She is terrified, but she knew she had to do it. Because you know what? She has finally, had 'enough.'"

I was stunned. Something about his story, this simple analogy, hit me square in the gut.

And I knew in my heart of hearts, he was right. I had already fought extremely hard to reach weight restoration. I was doing all of this for *something*, even if the distorted thoughts of anorexia were currently clouding my judgement. For a few moments, I was able to reach myself again- the logical side of me that knew I needed to pick myself back up, and continue onward.

I've been extremely independent, my entire life. I never needed anyone's help because I was so used to doing everything for myself, *by* myself- I actually preferred it that way.

And that was exactly my problem.

I was still turning to my eating disorder when I should have been reaching out for help. I was waiting until I reached crisis mode to talk to anyone about what was going on. I was using self-destructive behaviors, when I should have been using my words.

Was I instantly cured that day? No. Did I refrain from *all* behaviors after that one powerful discussion? Not exactly. The road to eating disorder recovery is long and complicated. I wish I could say that I was immediately healed from that moment forward. Sometimes, we have the greatest intentions and motivations, yet we still fall short—such is being human.

I ended up getting "enough" tattooed on my ankle, with the hope of never forgetting my epiphany in his office-- the moment when I conceded to my innermost self that I was a fighter; a brave warrior in a seemingly impossible battle. Little by little, I practiced relinquishing the control that I had clung to as my saving grace.

"She said she was willing to make up the snack she missed, but not for what she discarded at lunch. She said she would ask for it herself."

It wasn't a perfect resolve to our discussion, but it felt like a pretty good start to me.

i'

....

Panic Attacks

"NOW, IF SOME panic hits me, you have to sort of be friends with your body."

– Ellie Goulding

A Thread Unraveling

Monica Reagan

IN 2002, MY DAD WENT to prison and I became highly depressed. I hid it from everyone—my family, friends, coworkers. I had to be strong and help hold up my family with support. I struggled with stomach issues, sleeping all the time, not wanting to eat, and I had no energy or desire to do anything. I even stopped talking to friends. I struggled to go to work and was happy to get back to my apartment, where I felt safe and could hide from the world. Eventually, this didn't work. I was in graduate school for counseling—and I should have known, but wasn't ready to acknowledge: I... had... depression. Me? Really?

I tried antidepressants to no avail; side effects for all of them I was not happy with. I started using the skills I was learning in graduate school. I changed my diet, began walking, and talked to my friends and mom about what was going on. I was not prepared to let everyone know, just those close to me. I asked them to encourage me to get out of the house and to invite me to events and not take "no" for an answer. Perseverance worked and my depression slowly stopped controlling my life. I started feeling happy again; like myself. This didn't happen overnight, it took weeks, no, months. My life began to knit back together, one thread at a time. I was proud of myself. I had done it! Bye depression. I could relate to what graduate school, the books and professors were telling me. I was on the right track. This is what I was meant to do. Finally, an "aha" moment in my life.

Dad got out in 2007 and our family had an amazing few months—the best in my life. Then the worst. Mom died unexpectedly in November 2007. My entire life turned upside down. How could this happen? My mom was my best friend. My family was falling apart without answers; only sorrow. Oh no—here comes the depression again. I was unraveling a thread at a time. This time was different. I couldn't sleep, eat, or think, my mind racing all the time, and I was afraid of everything and of everyone dying. I felt like a zombie all day and night. Every. Single. Day. Most of those days I don't remember. I slept at other people's houses or someone stayed with me. I remember the funeral home and the celebration ceremony, which I sang at, but don't recall much else. How did I even sing? The next day was Thanksgiving and I stayed up all night with my best friend making pies, dumplings, peeling potatoes. Did I sleep? I can't recall—the next few weeks are still a complete blur. Just unraveling.

Immediately after Mom died, my doctor prescribed me Xanax. I took it but initially I didn't feel any better. How was I supposed to be feeling? What was I supposed to do? Going back to work was awful. I couldn't focus, my mind raced, each client story hit me hard. I left work for another week. What I did that week, I have no clue. My friends and I had planned on running a 5K for St. Jude's and it would be my first and last. What I didn't expect was what happened next. We were running past the hospital where mom died and I couldn't stop staring at it—I couldn't breathe, I couldn't see, I couldn't move. I was frozen. I was dying. What was happening to me? I got hot and sweaty and I could feel my heart nearly coming out of my chest. My best friend was talking to me, but I didn't know what she was saying. She stood by me until I snapped back into reality. I don't recall the rest of the day, but I was scared, fearful. I went to my doctor after having this feeling several more times. I thought I was having a heart attack, but all tests were normal—except my heart rate was ridiculously high. Panic Attack. What? Me? I had overcome depression. Give me a break please. Anxiety and panic attacks? I'm not dying? Sure feels like it and no one understands what's going on inside my body and my mind. Come on—not me.

I was sure there was something medical going on. So, I started meds again. But it was no overnight fix. I was feeling hopeless. This wasn't going to work. I had to start using what I learned in school, and practice what I was preaching to my clients and to my staff. *Deep breathing, counting, relaxation.* It was all bullshit—it wasn't working for me!

After several long weeks, I started to see the difference. I could sleep without fearing my family would die. I didn't feel my heart about to come out of my chest or burst into pieces. It was a long, slow process. Since then, I have decreased my meds, stopped, increased, and even changed meds. I no longer need some of them because I've learned to cope effectively (still not deep breathing, it doesn't work for me, but it can and does for so many others). I still have times where I don't want to do things because I'm too nervous. I become anxious at odd times and in odd places for no reason. I haven't had panic attacks in a while, but my anxiety still runs high and often. I've stopped checking my heart rate, because it has only caused more anxiety. I'm working on it every day. One thread at a time.

Just recently I have been able to truly open up to anyone and everyone about my struggles. I'm just now confident to do so. It's funny how I can teach, say and encourage others to do what I couldn't do before. Now I'm learning. One day, and some days, one minute, at a time.

Masculinity in Emotion

Chase Skopek

A JUMBLED COLLECTION OF tattered pages and scratched out words, hard to read and even harder to comprehend. It is seldom told, in fear that those who are listening will want nothing more than to erase it from their memories and toss it back on the shelf. On September 18th, 2015, I tried to kill myself. I was fifteen years old. This is the story I thought I wouldn't be alive to write.

I often questioned why I felt the way I did. I had good grades, I excelled in sports. The stigma around depression forbade me to suffer, I am privileged, *there is nothing to be sad about.* I loved my friends and was the life of every party, so when I stopped going out, they started asking why. I cut them off mid-sentence and assured them I was just, busy. I didn't have time to socialize any-more. Which was true, I was engrossed in hosting my own party. One inside of my head, where self-doubt danced with insecurity, depression mingled with anxiety. My brain soon became the pi-ñata and each of them had a turn to swing at it, in hopes I would finally break.

Panic and anxiety are those two weird friends that always show up to places in which they are not welcome, even though depres-sion extended them an invitation. I was now too anxious to ask my friends to hangout and too depressed to go, even if they had said yes. Panic and anxiety disorder forced me to channel the art-ist inside of myself. The wall, the mirrors, and the door as the canvas, my fist as the brush, and the blood trickling down my hands as paint. Sean Landers, a fellow artist, spoke truthfully in one of his paintings that read, "True artists kill themselves at their peak to prevent themselves from making bad work." I'm not sure which piece was my best, maybe after falling asleep and wak-ing up to the holes in my wall with the sound of my father scream-ing, I realized my greatest work had already been made.

The first time I thought of suicide, I was at a party, along with fifty others. I was trapped with words sitting on my tongue, too scared to leave my mouth. Drowning in a sea of teenage bodies had never made me feel more alone. The broken ladder to social acceptance was too hard to climb and I guess you could say that I almost died trying. I became infatuated with the idea of myself lying in a casket or bottled up in an urn; most people fear death, but I feared living. The realization that I have control over whether I live or die came almost as an epiphany. I made the de-cision to kill myself, and there was no stopping me.

I devised a plan, strategic and obtainable. Scrawling my final words onto paper was the first time I had genuinely smiled in as long as I could remember. I was finally at peace. My family's grief after losing me had to be incomparable to my own mental torture. I had been a burden anyway, right? I stood on the bathroom floor, barefoot and cold, holding an entire bottle of painkillers that I had so elaborately planned to swallow. I finally had control. I poured them into the palm of my hand, and swallowed them with vengeance.

I imagined my suicide as the tranquil slip away that I had replayed in my head over and over. It was nothing like that. The moment I realized that my life could be over, the peace I imagined was gone, and regret took its place. How was I going to look the woman that gave me this life in the face and tell her that I tried to end it? I knew I needed to tell her, so I mustered all of the courage I had and told my mother I had tried to kill myself.

After two days in the hospital, I was transported to a behavioral health hospital, and put in an adolescent unit with teenagers similar to me. I realized I spent my whole life worrying so much about others, that I forgot to worry about myself. I learned that when mental illness becomes unbearable, it's okay to be a little selfish. This disease is a monster, that sometimes hides in the shadows and other times breathes down your neck, waiting to consume you. I fight every day to keep it where it belongs, hidden within my shadow, I know that it will always be there, but I refuse to let *it* control *me*.

I have good days; I have bad days. I have really good days and really bad days. The road to happiness is long and filled with bumps, but I keep on driving, uncertain of my destination. I often ask myself, what is the price of happiness? My parents have relentlessly tried to fix me, but then I remind myself that I don't need to be fixed because I am not broken. People are confused when they hear of my mental illness, rather surprised. Just because I have projected myself onto others as the carefree student athlete, does not devalue my depression. Anyone can suffer, and every day I serve as *living* proof. My depression has not only taught me the brutal reality of mental illness, but it has also taught those who are willing to listen. As an adolescent male, I used to be scared to convey emotion of any kind. Emotion does not emasculate anyone, it is empowering. Defying social constructs gives me yet another reason to keep fighting. I'm grateful to have witnessed the beauty this world has to offer, despite its brief moments of agony. Thankfully each day is a new page, every accomplishment a new chapter. My story is far from over and I am beyond grateful I have the chance to keep writing it.

Be Still my Beating Heart

Lauren Wolfson

A S A LONG TIME *Lion King* lover I was thrilled when my high school theatre guild announced that there would be a field trip to a professional theatre to see it performed live. As I sat in the theatre I could feel the buzz of the crowd around me as the lights dimmed and the overture began. I was in a trance for most of the first act until (spoiler alert) Scar kills Simba. My heart started to beat in time with the maddening tempo of the music and I started to hyperventilate, not a normal reaction to a great piece of theatre. Blindly searching the shadowed theater, I manually ticked off each of my breaths and tried to calm myself down to no avail. I stood up and made my way from the middle of the row past annoyed patrons until I got to the door to the hallway.

"How can I help you?" the kind usher asked me. I couldn't manage to string two words together until I muttered, "I don't feel well," and then waited in the lobby until the show was over.

I told my friends that I left because I got sick but I had no words for what I had experienced. I was still breathing but terrified that I was going to die or float up into space or disappear into thin air. I thought the feeling would subside eventually so I asked a friend to borrow her iPod. The music helped but I still felt dreadful when the bus pulled up to my school. From that day on I struggled with breathing and near constant anxiety. It was as if there was a buzz in the back of my brain that would never shut off. I would sit in class digging my nails into my palms to anchor myself. It never once occurred to me that this was something other people were dealing with or that there was any way to alleviate the pain. I thought that I would be miserable for the rest of my life.

My anxiety came to a peak when I went away to college. I barely ate or drank and cried all the time. I lost twenty pounds almost instantly. I was desperate for a solution and was put on medication and started seeing a therapist. Things improved for a while and though I had thought I reached rock bottom during my freshman year, I was wrong.

During my junior year, I went to Paris, France. The days leading up to the two-week trip were spent in mess of anxiety and I felt like I had a brick in my stomach. When I arrived at the airport I began to cry hysterically and didn't event want to go on the trip until my brother convinced me. Once I was in Paris I only ate when I was with my group and even then it was very little and I got maybe an hour of sleep a night. I ended up leaving after three days because my anxiety got dangerously high. I thought after getting home I would be back to my pre-Paris levels of anxiety. I was wrong.

I began to have mini panic attacks, which occurred more regularly than before, but the worst part was the depression and suicidal thoughts that occurred on a daily basis. I started seeing a therapist again and after a month, thankfully, the suicidal thoughts subsided.

Later that year, I was in church one day when I realized why I was given anxiety—to help others. I began speaking openly about my mental health condition and started making YouTube videos on every mental hardship I had been through. I was thrilled to get messages that people were responding well to my videos and feeling like they weren't alone.

I grew more determined and started a mental health organization on my college campus where we had weekly meetings to check in with one another and brainstorm ways to reach out and help others. I also started taking time out of my day to check in with people and be an ear for those who struggle. People are grateful to have someone they can talk to who doesn't make them feel crazy. In conversations with people I am very open about my mental illness as well as the fact that I go to therapy. While therapy is not an appealing idea to everyone, I treat it like taking my brain to the gym for a workout.

Sometimes I have bad days, but that doesn't mean I have a bad life. My favorite quote that helps me through the worst of times comes from Isaiah 41:10. "So do not fear, for I am with you; do not be dismayed, for I am your God. I will strengthen you and help you; I will uphold you with my righteous right hand." Every day God's hand guides me through my anxiety so I can hold out a helping hand to others, and that's the biggest blessing of them all.

i'

....

Obsessive Compulsive Disorder

"OCD IS LIKE having a bully stuck inside your head and nobody else can see it."

- Krissy McDermott

The Strength Within

Britt Berlin

T'S ALWAYS DISORIENTING waking up in an unfamiliar place. The morning after I attempted to take my life, I couldn't quite place where I was for the first few moments. The room was sterile, but not like your standard hospital room. The four walls encompassing me were adorned in faded yellow wallpaper. Old, floor-length curtains framed the single locked window that peered out into the parking lot. Two beds with a thin white sheet guarded a muted peach bedside table; a small stack of papers including my rights (or lack thereof) as a patient, hospital schedule, and meal choices resting on top. The tip of the sun was just kissing the horizon, but the sky was still fighting to stay asleep in a dark haze. I was in the psych ward.

It was a new day, but all I felt was emptiness. The night before, I had fallen asleep rocking back and forth on the bed and clutching my knees to try to soften my tormented sobs.

Another patient, or rather, a fellow inmate, walked by and screamed into my room, "Quit your crying, blondie! You'll get used to it." I cried even harder. I cried until I felt numb from exhaustion rather than pain.

That morning, before anyone else was awake, I just lied there in bed, still feeling so much and yet absolutely and unbearably nothing at all. That's what depression will do to you. I chalked this attempt at suicide as just another one of my failures in life, just another reason why I didn't deserve to live. But at this point, I didn't know if I still wanted death. I just wanted an out. I wanted an escape from this hell that was inside my head and the prison I was surrounded by. In that moment, I was struck with a deep desire to be a child again and make it all disappear. I was twenty-years-old at the time, and all I wanted was my mom.

How does one get to this point, though? I thought, staring blankly at the ceiling of the psych ward. How the hell did I get here? What went wrong? Once a girl of confidence, strength, and stubbornness to a fault, I found myself groveling on the floor of the hospital.

"I'll be good, I'll be good! Please just let me go!" I had pleaded with the hospital staff that night, my shrieks drowning out the other patients in the Emergency Room.

This was not the beginning, nor was it the end, of my struggle with mental illness. At age ten, I was diagnosed with Obsessive Compulsive Disorder (OCD), which later led to being comorbid with anorexia nervosa. Just when I thought I was coming out of the darkness of my eating disorder, depression sucked me back in. It fooled me into thinking that everything that I believed to be true was just the opposite. Once in love with mornings, I dreaded leaving my bed, wishing that one day, I just wouldn't wake up. I used to consider myself an artist, but when I was depressed, I refused to pick up a paintbrush because depression stole my love for painting and drawing. I stopped talking to my therapist and nutritionist, both of whom I had known since I was twelve years old, thinking that any help was pointless because I was not going to get better. I soon believed that everyone—my friends, family, and fellow classmates—hated me, and that I was worth absolutely nothing. Depression had tricked me into thinking that I was worthless and a waste of space. It robbed me of my will to live.

This is what depression does.

But it took facing depression and a near-death experience for me to realize that even though depression can do all that, I was still stronger; the real Brittany was still alive and well and willing to fight because life *is* beautiful, and I was so much more than what depression was telling me. And so, my fight against depression began, one that started with me and only me, and then grew into a support system beyond my imagination.

Not every day was and is a success, however. I had set backs, and still do. Some days, I felt on top of the world, and my flame of hope was not a flicker, but rather a blaze of fire. Other days, I found myself crying on the floor, wondering why I was wasting everyone's time and fearing that I would never get better. But even on those bad days, I amazed myself in finding more strength than I ever thought possible.

On one particular bad day during recovery, I reached out to a friend who also suffered from depression, and he told me this: "Out of the days you've lived so far, you have had a one hundred percent success rate. You have completed each day and have made it to the next." He was right. While every day is not great, there is good and love in each day, and you deserve to see that. It may not get easier, but you get stronger. That strength makes all the difference.

Life on the Other Side of Fear

Autumn Aurelia

NEVER IMAGINED I'D LIVE PAST twenty. Looking back to my teenage years, I battled with suicidal thoughts on a daily basis and I was certain that my life would be a short one.

My every minute was spent living in fear; fear of losing my mom, fear of dying, fear of living, blood, bodily functions, my environment, germs and being poisoned. Everywhere I looked, fear loomed from the darkest and the brightest corners.

Unlike all of the others which came and went, one particularly traumatic fear has stayed with me my entire life.

Mom and I were laying side by side on her bed, just like we used to do most nights. The radio was playing softly in the background while she caressed the tips of my hair. We were inseparable and then we weren't.

"On tonight's show we're going to be tackling the topic of childhood abuse," the radio host announced.

I froze. How I wish I could have scooped myself up from that bed so I would never hear those cruel, dangerous words—the words that changed my life forever: "Abused children always go on to abuse others."

That's when the fear hooked its teeth into me. "You're an abuser," it said. "You were abused so now you will go onto abuse others." I wanted to scream, kick, punch and fight my way out of this awful thought, but I couldn't. Once a thought existed in my mind, it was truth. *Fact.*

I left my mother's room that night a different girl. I was an adult now, an evil monster destined to do bad things. In the days that followed, I devised a plan that would help me live with this new reality. It wasn't a plan to "cure" me, though I later spent years seeking this—in religion, in people, in alcohol, self-harm and suicide attempts. My plan back then, however, was avoidance: I told myself that if I could avoid children, I would be okay. I would be okay because *they* would be safe. See, I never wanted to harm a child. On the contrary, I went out of my way to never see or talk to children.

As the years went on, my fear of harming children turned into something darker. I remember switching on the television one day and hearing news of a murder involving two children. They had been raped first. This acted as food for my already tortured imagination. Not only did I fear becoming a child abuser, I now believed that I would murder children too. I believed that I had murdered and abused *those* two children, even though the incident took place hundreds of miles away. I had no transport, and most importantly no memory of ever harming, abusing or killing anyone. Despite this, I still walked past my local police station a dozen times a day for weeks on end, wondering if I should hand myself in for a crime I didn't remember playing any part in.

As the years went on, these fears became far stronger, as did the "false memories." The four years I spent at university were among the most difficult years of my life. Each night, I'd lock myself away by dragging large pieces of furniture across my bedroom floor.

Cupboard in place?

Check.

Desk in place?

Check.

Chair in place?

Check.

It seemed logical to me that if I couldn't trust myself during my waking hours, I should be extra cautious while sleeping. *What if I do something bad during the night and don't remember it?* With all furniture pushed against the door, I felt a little safer that I wouldn't "escape." This setup gave me a false sense of protection, acting as a barrier between my thoughts and the danger I believed myself to be.

Ashamed, I kept all of this darkness locked away from others, burying it deep within me, where no one would ever be able to find it.

Like I said, I never expected to live past twenty, so when I reached twenty-eight and I was still living this tortured, broken life, I felt it was time to give up. I had no answers as to why I feared myself, why I was experiencing such horrid thoughts or how I would survive them. I needed this enduring battle with my mind to be over, so one night I started taking pills—lots of them. But in a final moment of desperation, I reasoned with my mind long enough to ask, "what if." What if there is a cure for me? What if I'm not a child abuser after all? I opened my laptop and Googled: "I'm scared I will abuse children."

The results directed me to an article on Pure O, which outlined the reality of an illness called obsessive-compulsive disorder—an illness often mocked and belittled by society. "Could I really have OCD?" I asked myself. I didn't clean, and I wasn't organised. I spent hours reading about OCD and found that there was so much more to this disorder. It is intrusive thinking, obsessions and compulsions. It's fear of harming others, fear of your own mind, of losing control. It described me perfectly.

And just as the corners of my world folded in on me all of those years ago when I was fourteen, they finally unfolded at twenty-eight, and for the first time since it all began, I could see a spark of hope.

I went to see my doctor and was diagnosed with severe OCD, though my biggest breakthrough hasn't been diagnosis or recovery. I'm not there yet. I am housebound and still living with the fear of harming children, except now that fear has a name.

My greatest breakthrough came when I started speaking out about OCD; that's the moment I began to heal. That's why I believe recovery should be shared, and it is our stories that ultimately help others.

i'

....

Learning to be a Better Parent to a Child with OCD

Chris Baier

S THE SUMMER OF 2013 BEGAN, my daughter, Vanessa, suddenly became a completely different girl. In the span of a few days, she went from a happy-go-lucky eight-year-old too timid, frightened and overly anxious.

She refused to leave the house, started asking repetitive questions about germs and illness, and wouldn't eat anything without first checking the ingredients or expiration date.

As June turned to July, things got worse. Vanessa became a nervous wreck prone to emotional outbursts. She could burst into tears or start screaming depending on what was bothering her.

{ 225 }

My wife and I became increasingly confused and worried. We knew Vanessa needed help. She even asked to see a therapist.

So, we had her evaluated by a child psychologist who specialized in anxiety. Soon the diagnosis came back: Obsessive Compulsive Disorder (OCD).

This news sent our family scrambling in multiple directions. We made it our mission to understand OCD. We read books, joined online parenting groups, and eventually started our own local support group.

Vanessa started meeting with a therapist trained in Exposure and Response Prevention_(ERP). ERP is the most effective type of Cognitive Behavioral Therapy (CBT) for people with OCD. She began learning how her brain worked, what made OCD evil and doing exposures that would help her take back control.

At the same time, my wife and I began our journey of discovery, frustration, success and advocacy. We learned a lot along the way so I wanted to jot down some of these "lessons learned" through my first 4 years of trial and error, failing and understanding. These realizations made me a better parent to a child with a mental health issue. They also helped me maintain my sanity.

You are Not Alone

This is the most powerful sentence a child suffering from OCD can hear.

I know this because every child interviewed for my OCD documentary mentioned it.

I know this because the day Vanessa really started to get better was the day she met a girl her age with OCD and realized she wasn't alone. Her progress then skyrocketed after she joining a group therapy program with other kids struggling with OCD.

Mental health disorders are isolating. Kids withdraw and get lonely. They believe, and may verbalize, that no one else is "like me."

Vanessa's number one concern initially was that other kids would find out. So a key thing I did was search for videos, stories and books that involved real tweens with OCD. I shared everything I found. Eventually it sunk in and she felt accepted.

The lesson I learned: the spark of recovery can begin once your child understands they are not alone.

The Future is Tomorrow's Problem

As I processed Vanessa's OCD diagnosis, my mind drifted to focusing on, "What will this mean for her future?"

But I realized that worrying about what a mental health disorder may mean for Vanessa in ten, twenty or fifty years caused more stress than it's worth. That future is so far off, why waste brain cells thinking about it?

I needed to make the future (marriage, college, family, whatever) tomorrow's problem. I had to share this expectation with my family members and friends so they, too, would stop fixating on "What if." My energy, everyone's energy, was better spent dealing with the now—today, this week, this month. After all, this was the time we dedicated to kick OCD's butt.

The lesson for me: Focusing on how to help my child fight an obsession now. It made life easier than thinking about what may, or may not, happen years from now.

"Normal" is a Setting on a Washing Machine

When you find out your child has a mental health disorder, it's natural to wish he or she could be just like other kids. But the search for normal stops you from focusing on what's truly important—helping your child to overcome crippling rituals and compulsions.

Thinking back, my wish for "normal" was a grasp for stability. It wasn't that I hoped Vanessa would be like others, it's that I wanted her to be able to have a sleepover without an OCD worry frightening her so much she begged to come home.

For this to work, I had to stop thinking about the nebulous concept of "normal." I put normal where it belongs—as a setting on a washing machine. The lesson here: Concentrate on a real objective: helping kids overcome the OCD obstacles holding them back.

My Child Needs Help... but so Do I

The more we learned about OCD, the more my wife and I realized we needed support. There are things about this disorder and treatment that family and close friends just don't understand.

So we found support and a community that was experienced in the OCD rollercoaster and wouldn't be quick to judge our questions, concerns or ERP homework.

There are loads of ways to get help: OCD books, a therapist, or a private group on Yahoo or Facebook. The places and people that would let me share openly, and wouldn't sugarcoat their responses, were the ones I stuck with. You need tough love along with understanding.

The lesson I learned: don't be afraid to get help. You're a better parent and caregiver when you're mentally healthy.

Uncovering the OCD
Kari Ferguson

DON'T KNOW IF ANY OF US wants to be different. Not really. Not at first. It's once we have accepted the undeniable fact that there is something out of the ordinary that we begin to embrace the truth. Of course, acceptance of what is out of the ordinary isn't that cut and dry. It can take years. Believe me. I know.

Since you don't really have anything to judge against, you grow up thinking that you are normal. You figure that everyone is like this, and when you realize that they aren't, you hide. You cover up. You start collecting labels.

For me, it was that I was shy. A listener. An observer. Smart. Quiet. Eventually, our labels combine into a mosaic of a person. We became our labels until something more powerful rips them away. Sometimes that happens over time, and sometimes it comes with dramatic change, a huge stressor, or a life altering event.

By college, I had embraced my labels and moved to Seattle. I thought living alone would be ideal for me. But I wasn't alone. I brought along a mental illness that I didn't know I had. It fed on the stress. It relished in my loneliness. And it terrified me.

Unfortunately, I didn't recognize what it was at the time. I saw a doctor and took medication to shut it up. It wasn't until years later, when it took on a different and more recognizable face, that I finally recognized it for what it was—not anxiety, not anger problems, not health issues, not "craziness"—but obsessive compulsive disorder.

That's the thing about mental illness. Because most people don't want to talk about, acknowledge, or accept it, it remains stigmatized. Mental illnesses are pushed into the dark recesses of the closet of conversation. Without conversation and awareness, mass media mental illness prevails. We know only what is broadcast. We are familiar with the stereotypes rather than the realities.

It was when I found myself having to wash and rewash my hands, worrying about contamination, needing safe spaces to sit, and freaking out about germs, that it clicked, but still not completely. It wasn't until I found myself in a group therapy session for OCD that I realized that my current episode wasn't the beginning of my obsessive compulsive disorder but a flare up of a long standing relationship with the illness. I just didn't know until then how many faces OCD had.

I blubbered my way through that group session. The floodgates had broken. All my worries about copyright violation from burning CDs, anxiety over jaywalking or going over the speed limit, fears that I had hit others' cars with mine, stress over grading my students fairly, concerns about getting people ill... these were all symptoms of OCD.

Suddenly here were people who understood! Here they were, sitting around me in a small room, giving me a tissue and holding my hand as I struggled through tears. Ten or so years of my life began to make sense as I acknowledged and recognized what had been the problem all along. I felt the kind of hope and dismay you feel at the beginning of what is going to be a long and difficult journey to where you need to be.

The dismay definitely came more frequently than the hope. Mental illness doesn't go down without a fight, and my OCD certainly came out with gloves on. I went back on medication to give myself an upper hand. I undertook regular sessions with a psychologist. I carried on through sickness, bleeding hands, a move to be closer to good care, debilitating obsessions and exhausting compulsions. I learned how to face my anxiety and stay with it. I struggled with purposeful exposures to put myself in situations I feared and then not do what I thought would make me feel better. I persisted. I gained ground.

I vividly recall one drive home from the psychologist when I realized that I could have my life back. That shocking idea gave me the hope I so desperately needed. I didn't have to feel like life was too difficult anymore. Mental illness tries to convince you that every day will be more of the same. I had been under the impression that yes, I could struggle through each day, but for what?

Suddenly, I saw through that lie. I could and would regain control of my life. I would take myself back from the obsessive compulsive disorder. But how? By not listening. By fighting every obsession and resisting each compulsion. Would I be perfect? No. Would I ever be cured? Nope. But I could still live. I could be happy. I would be happy.

Not only that, but I wanted give others that vision. I had to try and increase awareness of mental illness. I didn't want others to go ten years without knowing what they were fighting against. Sure, maybe a diagnosis is just a label, but at least it comes with a plan, and that plan involves resources and hope for a new future.

It's when those of us with diagnoses speak up against the stigmas of mental illness that others are better able to find their own voice. They can find their own diagnoses as well as the courage to get help for themselves.

While stigma still persists, hope falters—and unfortunately, stigma will persist as long as we keep quiet and let stereotypes run the mental health conversation. Of course, speaking out brings judgment. Some people think I'm making a big deal out of something that doesn't really matter. Others wonder how I can't have anything better to do with my time.

Well, you know what? Increasing awareness and respect for mental health problems is one of the best ways I could spend my time. It's through being open that we can properly acknowledge our own issues, find help, and provide support for others—and those are the things that really matter.

i'

····································

Your i'Mpossible Story

(You)

Author Biographies

Stephen L. Mandel, M.D. is the founder and president of Ketamine Clinics of Los Angeles. He is a board-certified anesthesiologist with a master's degree in psychology who has been practicing medicine for over thirty-five years with extensive experience in the provision of anesthesia in both inpatient and outpatient settings for adults and children. He is an internationally recognized pioneer, using IV Ketamine Infusion Therapy for the treatment of depression, other mood disorders, and chronic pain conditions. Dr. Mandel has administered over 4,000 infusions since opening Ketamine Clinics of Los Angeles in 2014. ketamineclinics.com

Shannon Ackerman is in the high school graduating class of 2018. She loves dogs, tacos, and the color orange. She hopes to travel the world and help all those around her. Shannon likes to watch bad movies to make fun of them and enjoys springtime.

Nate Crawford is the Executive Director of Here/Hear, a nonprofit that works to give hope to those with mental illness and their loved ones. He is a regular contributor to The Mighty and blogs at www.herehear.org.

Reece Anderson is a married father of two who currently resides in Brisbane, Australia. Reece's passion is in coaching and mentoring others while sharing his experiences in overcoming debilitating anxiety, depression, and tics (involuntary body movements). After growing tired of the side effects brought on by taking various prescription medications, Reece made a decision to stop taking the drugs he had been prescribed for fifteen years and seek alternative treatment. Reece is now eighteen months medication-free and is in the best mental and physical shape of his life. Reece is an advocate for alternatives treatments for anxiety and depression. reeceanderson.com.au

Tanya J. Peterson, NCC has been a teacher and counselor and now is a mental health writer and speaker. She writes for HealthyPlace.com: a weekly article on the *Anxiety-Schmanxiety* blog, the main article of their weekly newsletter, two e-books, and over 100 different articles throughout their website. She has also written four award-winning, critically-acclaimed mental health themed novels: *Losing Elizabeth, Leave of Absence, My Life in a Nutshell: a Novel,* and *Twenty-Four Shadows.*

Kendal Kooreny was Lyme disease in 2014 and was then inspired to explore happiness through a healthy lifestyle and, of course, while wearing high heels! She experimented with nutritious foods in the kitchen and discovered a new world filled with wonderful flavors! Photographing her journey as her passion for health grew, she desired to share her original recipes and healthy restaurant and product reviews with others...thus, the birth of Kendal's blog and brand, "Health and High Heels." You can find Health and High Heels on Instagram (@healthandhighheels), Facebook (Health and High Heels), Twitter (@healthhighheels), Pinterest (@healthhighheels), and Kendal's website (Healthandhighheels.org).

Penny Williams is an award-winning author, blogger, journalist, and speaker. She mentors parents raising kids with ADHD and/or autism. She's the parent of a son with ADHD and autism, and the author of three award-winning books on parenting kids with ADHD: *Boy Without Instructions, What to Expect When Parenting Children with ADHD,* and *The Insider's Guide to ADHD.* Penny is the current editor of ParentingADHDandAutism.com, Founder and Instructor for The Parenting ADHD & Autism Academy, and a frequent contributor on parenting and raising children with ADHD for ADDitude Magazine, Healthline, WNC Parent, and other parenting and special needs publications.

Cristina Margolis is a passionate advocate for ADHD (Attention Deficit Hyperactivity Disorder), particularly in children. She is the founder of My Little Villagers, a website with stories, resources, and recommendations for families with ADHD. Her writing has been featured in *ADDitude Magazine,* as well as on popular websites, such as ADDitude, The Mighty, and Scary Mommy. She also runs a worldwide pen pal program for children with ADHD called Pen Pallies and plans on creating more programs to help families with ADHD. You can follow her family's journey with ADHD on Facebook, Twitter, YouTube, and at www.mylittlevillagers.com

Jessica Jurkovic is a critical-care nurse, freelance writer, and fierce mental health advocate. She is the founder and writer at Hackrack.org, a website dedicated to helping families and individuals affected by ADHD. She lives in the Chicagoland area and is the proud with her amazing husband and four very beautiful, very active children.

Brianna Miedema is a junior at a Christian High School in a small town in Iowa. She is very involved in the arts at her school such as the band, orchestra, and play. She enjoys writing in her English class, but also writing blog posts for The Mighty. She writes mainly on her struggles with her depression and self-harm. Brianna's hope in writing about her battles is not only to experience healing, but to more importantly spread awareness in her community and let others who are struggling with the same things feel like they are not alone.

Mary Sukala is a twenty-year-old freelance writer with a softspot for mental health advocacy. Taking the pain and spinning it into something that could save a life makes it immensely rewarding for her. Sukala's work has been featured on xoJane, Thought Catalog, and the front page of The Mighty. Whether she is tinkering around on her blog, *The Deep End Diaries*, or the never ending stack of other projects, language is always on her mind. Still in the green years of her career, she hopes to take the wordsmithing world by storm with her candidness, humor, and, unfailing passion.

Ashley Lewis Carroll is a mother to two school-age daughters, wife to the Father of Every Year, social worker in the domestic and sexual violence field by day, and writer in the wee hours of occasional mornings. Ashley posts the momentous and the minutiae of her life on Instagram and is resurrecting her blogger identity at ashleylewiscarroll.com. Ashley has been published on Elephant Journal, Scary Mommy, Feminine Collective, and The Mighty.

Timothy Cyron is a junior at Xavier University. He is majoring in psychology and minoring in theology. He hopes to become and clinical psychologist and work with youth and adolescents struggling with mental illness. Timothy enjoys, exercising, reading, and writing poetry and rap. They all help him cope with his mental illnesses. Timothy has one older sister and two younger sisters. His family resides in Los Altos California. Timothy hopes to return to California after he receives his undergraduate degree and go to graduate school closer to home.

Caitlin McLaughlin is a pre-junior in a 5-year BA/MA program in English and Publishing at Drexel University. She works as the Digital Communications Co-op for Drexel Publishing Group, where she fields submissions for *Painted Bride Quarterly* literary magazine. Caitlin's writing has been featured on *Stigma Fighters*, a blog dedicated to mental health visibility.

Michelle Graffeo is a Certified Peer Support Specialist, a Recovery Support Group Facilitator for both NAMI as well as BRIDGES, and a WRAP facilitator for the Copeland Center. She lives in Denham Springs, Louisiana with her wife and two teenage boys, Julius and Maxie. Michelle struggled with both depression and addiction for over twenty years and is now coming up on her fourth year of sobriety. Her lives goal is to help others who are also struggling with mental illness and addiction, to help reduce stigma, and to pass the message that recovery is possible.

Cynthia Mauzerall grew up in Maine the youngest of four siblings—having to act quickly to keep up with her big brothers and older sister. That quickness took her to Wake Forest University where she ran cross country and track and studied psychology. At Wake, Cynthia volunteered at a crisis hotline and an interest sparked in counseling. She obtained a master's degree in Clinical Psychology at Pepperdine and became a licensed counselor. After her brother's death by suicide in 2004, she became even more passionate about counseling and suicide prevention. She is Director of The Health and Wellness Center at the College of Idaho.

Estelle Matranga was born in Nice, France, and graduated from La Sorbonne-Nouvelle in Paris in 2010 with a major in Cinematography and a minor in Theatre. She studied acting in Paris and in Los Angeles after she moved in 2012. She now studies screenwriting at the Twin Bridges Screenwriting Salon and is currently writing her first screenplay. Estelle works as a Post Production Coordinator both in Visual Effects and Film Coloration. Another one of her passion is Dance and she never misses an opportunity to move her body to the rhythm of the music.

Amy Kay is of Laotian descent, originally from Orlando, Florida and currently living in Mobile, Alabama. She was diagnosed with schizophrenia in 2008. She is an active mental health advocate and through her blog Voice of a Schizophrenic, she takes her readers and followers on her journey through living with and managing her brain disorder. http://voiceofaschizophrenic.blogspot.com.

Victoria Marie Alonso was born and raised in Southern California and currently resides in California with her husband of twenty-four years and one of her three children. After her diagnosis with schizoaffective disorder, she earned her Master's Degree in psychology at Brandman University. She worked in the mental health field for four years with children who suffered from various mental disorders until stress caused a relapse of psychotic symptoms and decided to retire from the field. Victoria currently writes about her journey of recovery from Schizoaffective Disorder and has an active blog where she reaches people around the world.

Bethany Yeiser is an author and a dynamic communicator of the experience of severe, untreated schizophrenia and chronic homelessness. Her memoir *Mind Estranged* (2014) follows her trajectory from the onset of mental illness, through acute psychosis, homelessness, two brief incarcerations, and full recovery. As a motivational speaker, Bethany inspires positive change in the way people diagnosed with schizophrenia are characterized and treated in the health care system and by society. In July, 2016, Bethany became founding president of the CURESZ Foundation (Comprehensive Understanding via Research and Education into Schizophrenia). You can find her at www.bethanyyeiser.com.

August Pfizenmayer is a writer, blogger, and social media manager from Georgia. She studies English at the University of North Georgia. While writing about her experiences with mental illness is a valuable coping skill, she hopes to raise awareness, as well. The Mighty, The Odyssey, and Thought Catalog are a few of the websites where her writing has appeared. In her free time, August loves to go to bookstores and eat ice cream. Her latest project is a collection of poetry on Wattpad called, *Sinking into Psychosis*. You can also find her at Survival is a Talent, her personal blog.

Amy Oestreicher is a PTSD specialist, artist, author, writer for Huffington Post, TEDx and RAINN speaker, award-winning health advocate, actress and playwright—sharing the lessons learned from trauma through her writing, artwork, performance and speaking. She has headlined international conferences as a keynote speaker, and as author and star of *Gutless & Grateful,* her one-woman musical autobiography. Her writings have appeared in over seventy online and print publications, and her story has appeared on *TODAY,* "Cosmopolitan," and CBS. She's currently touring a mental health advocacy/sexual assault awareness program to colleges nationwide and developing her full-length PTSD drama, *Imprints.*

Matt Pappas publishes podcasts, videos, and writes regularly on his blog, SurvivingMyPast.net. He is driven to not only heal himself from this past abuse, but to do everything possible to inspire, encourage, support, and validate survivors everywhere.

Twitter: @SurvivingMyPast | Facebook.com/SurvivingMyPast | Instagram.com/SurvivingMyPast

Karen Strait is married to Richard Strait and has two sons. She has a Master's in Science in Clinical Counseling from Central Methodist University. Karen has a passion for suicide prevention and is currently in the process helping to organize an Out of the Darkness Walk. She also has a passion for helping parents who have lost children. Karen enjoys writing and is in process of putting a book together. She has been published in the Church Advocate, Christian Connection, Woman's World and Farmington Forum. She loves being around family. She is also an avid reader.

Candace Yoder is the executive director of the Matthew Silverman Memorial Foundation (MSMF), a non-profit organization in teen mental health awareness and suicide prevention. In her four years with MSMF, she has cultivated more than fifty school partners, training thousands of students, parents, educators, and faculty in mental health and suicide prevention. Candace is trained in the teacher's edition of emotional intelligence at Yale University's Center for Emotional Intelligence. She is currently being trained in the First Response Team for homicides in Los Angeles. She volunteers in prisons, educating inmates on the intersection of trauma and mental health.

Danielle Hark is a writer, freelance photographer and photo editor, and certified life coach whose work has been featured in various publications, including Psychology Today, Dr. Oz's YouBeauty, The Mighty, and Upworthy, as well as numerous books and anthologies. Danielle is also a mental health advocate who lives with depression, anxiety, and bipolar disorder. In the midst of her struggles, Danielle founded Broken Light Collective, a non-profit organization that empowers people living with or affected by mental illness using photography. www.Danielle-Hark.com | www.BrokenLightCollective.com

Fiona Kennedy is 30ish, married, and has two kids and two dogs. In 2013, she started the blog, "Sunny Spells & Scattered Showers,"—moving away from psychiatric diagnoses, one post at a time. http://sunnyspellsandscatteredshowers.org

Melissa Whelan was born in Shawville, Quebec and then raised in Les Appalaches (Appalachian) Regional County in Thetford Mines, Quebec. English is her mother tongue and she is fluent in *le français québécois* (Canadian French).

Benjamin Tyler is a transformational speaker and creator of Unleash Yourself—a program that has changed the lives of people across the world to stand in their potential. He believes that the path to living a fulfilled life is found through the meaning you derive from the work you do, relationships you build with others, and the relationship with one's self. You can learn more about Benjamin and his work by heading over to Benjamin-Tyler.com.

Lotta Dann is the author of the popular sober blog "Mrs. D Is Going Without." Her memoir of the same name was published three years after she got sober. She is the manager of the recovery community website Living Sober (www.livingsober.org.nz). She lives in Wellington, New Zealand with her husband, three sons and black labrador. She is currently working on her second book. livingwithoutalcohol.blogspot.com

Deeatra Kajfosz is an award-winning suicide awareness and prevention advocate, public speaker, and founder of LiFE OF HOPE, an organization responsible for a comprehensive approach to the prevention of suicide attempt and death. She reaches audiences with her story of hidden secrets, cycles of chronic major depression and anxiety, a near fatal suicide attempt, and an unexpected twist toward acceptance, healing, and hope for others. Today, Deeatra dedicates her life to raising awareness, providing education, and supporting others. It is through her own life journey that her story connects with her audience in highly personal and inspiring ways. DeeatraK.com

Imade Nibokun is a Columbia Non-Fiction MFA graduate who turned her Depressed While Black thesis into an in-progress book and online platform that shares mental health stories from an African-American lens. She writes about depression at the intersection of race, romance, and religion. Imade is also a freelance writer with published work in LA Weekly, VICE, Atlanta Journal Constitution, and WNYC.

Jeanine Hoff is the founder of Where is the Sunshine?, a non-profit organization and social media resource dedicated to positive mental health advocacy through education and community collaboration. Jeanine is a TEDx presenter on mental health, a certified presenter for the National Alliance on Mental Illness' (NAMI) Peer-to-Peer program, helped create Mental Health America's nationwide Peer Specialist Accreditation Certification team and is certified in Mental Health First Aid. She is a classically trained musician holding both a Bachelor's and Master's degree from Arizona State University. She and husband Mathew are the proud parents of three boys.

Miriam Ament is the founder and president of No Shame On U, a non-profit organization dedicated to eliminating the stigma associated with mental health conditions and raising awareness in the Jewish community and beyond. The goal is for the people who need help to seek it, for family members and friends to know how to provide proper support and to save lives. Miriam earned her B.A. in American History from Barnard College and a Master's in Organizational Psychology from Teachers College, Columbia University. She lives in Chicago with her husband, musician David Forman. www.noshameonu.org

Elaina J. Martin is passionate about stomping out the stigma of mental illness. She recently completed a memoir about living with mental illness that she hopes will one day end up in the hands of someone who needs a little hope. She writes the blog "Being Beautifully Bipolar" at PsychCentral.com and a personal blog at ElainaJ.com. When not writing or trying to snag a literary agent, she is the girlfriend to a charming Navy sailor and is a loving pet-parent to two big black dogs.

Cynthia Forget was diagnosed with bipolar disorder in 2005. Since then she has been through a myriad of experiences and treatments, and more than ten years later has finally reached a stable state—as stable as one can be with bipolar disorder. In 2014, she began a blog entitled *Real Life with Bipolar Disorder* (www.cynthiaforget.weebly.com). The purpose of her blog is to bring awareness to bipolar disorder and support for those who suffer from it. Through Facebook, Twitter, and her blog, she is a strong advocate for those with bipolar disorder. Cynthia lives and writes in Peterborough, Ontario, Canada.

Laura Marchildon lives in Ontario, Canada and is a writer and blogger with lived experience. She is an active advocate who raises awareness on mental health through her website Our Bipolar Family and through various social media platforms. Laura is also an accomplished book reviewer on the genre of Mental Health. www.ourbpfamily.org.

Kate Dolan is a free-spirited writer who lives in New York. Along with her meds and therapy, Kate uses CrossFit, meditation, and healthy eating to live a happy, healthy life. Kate has bipolar disorder type II and is no longer ashamed of it. https://thebrochick.com

Suzi Leigh is a mother of two living with depression and anxiety. After graduating with a degree in English, Suzi stayed home with her two sons and cherished those years before starting her own business in 2015. She has made it her life's work to empower women and mothers to take better care of themselves, and is a writer, entrepreneur, and postpartum support service. She lives with her two blonde-haired, blue-eyed boys, her husband of ten years, and two cats.

JoAnne Diaz is a happily married wife and mother to nine children ages eleven and under. When JoAnne is not being chased by her children she works part-time as a systems administrator. In JoAnne's "spare" time she blogs and writes books. You can follow JoAnne's adventures on Twitter, Facebook and on her blog Camaraderie Mom: www.camaraderiemom.com

Jen Schwartz is the founder and writer of the blog, The Medicated Mommy. After kicking postpartum depression's ass, she learned the importance of accepting herself as the mom she is (one who pops an antidepressant every morning and isn't having any more kids), not the mom she thought she was supposed to be (domestic goddess and Pinterest's mom of the year). Jen is an influencer at Mogul and a regular contributor at The Huffington Post, The Mighty, Motherlucker, and Suburban Misfit Mom. Her writing has also been featured on Scary Mommy, Mamalode, Postpartum Progress, Kveller, and Psych Meds. http://themedicatedmommy.com.

Heather Williams, BS, CCJP, MARS is a mental health and suicide prevention advocate who currently works as a Substance Abuse Specialist in an ITCD program. Heather graduated from Southeast Missouri State University with a degree in Psychology. She is currently enrolled in a Masters of Mental Health Counseling program at the same university. Heather sits on the board of the Eastern Missouri Chapter of the AFSP. She is a Mental Health First Aid Instructor. Heather is co-creator of listeningsaveslives.net in which she and her partner use their combination of clinical and lived experience to show how recovery is possible.

Molly Hillery is a writer, a teacher, and a mental health advocate. She has lived with mental illness most of her life, including depression and anxiety, PTSD, an eating disorder, addiction, and self-harm. She is the content coordinator and blog manager of a mental health organization called Where I Stand. By sharing her experience, she aims to provide hope to others that are struggling, to start important discussions, and to erase the stigma associated with mental illness. www.thisiswhereistand.org

Monica Reagan, MA, LPC, graduated from Southeast Missouri State University in 2005 with a Master of Arts in Community Counseling. She worked as a community support worker, crisis worker, assessor, and therapist while achieving her license. Monica became a Licensed Professional Counselor in 2007. She currently supervises a team of community support workers and is the QMHP for the integrated treatment for co-occurring disorders program. Monica is passionate about suicide prevention, Out of Darkness Walks, and advocating for mental health awareness. Monica lives in Cape Girardeau, Missouri.

Chase Skokep is an alleged old soul, hip hop enthusiast, and lover of all things adventurous and new. He is a high school junior, residing in McHenry, Illinois, a small suburb of Chicago. He is heavily involved in academics and is excited that this incredible project is only the start of his career and future as a writer. He is surrounded by an amazing family and friends, who continue to learn and understand his mental illness willingly. He is outspoken, unapologetic, and plans to spend his professional life as an activist for mental health and social justice.

Lauren Wolfson is a college senior whose role model is her mom. When not on stage signing or acting you can find her geeking out over "Harry Potter" or *The Phantom of the Opera*. She is involved in multiple organizations on campus and her favorite song is "I Dreamed a Dream" from the musical "Les Miserables" and book is "Pride and Prejudice". If she could change anything about the world she would eradicate Mental Illness. Her proudest accomplishments are being support for people who need her. The best way to make her happy is to take her to Disney World.

Britt Berlin is a recent graduate from Georgetown University and wannabe New Yorker. A copywriter by day and painter by night, Britt fills her free time running around New York City, writing to create awareness about depression, OCD, and eating disorders, doing yoga, learning how to cook (and not burn) dinner with her boyfriend, and playing with her cats. She lives by the motto: Still I rise.

Autumn Aurelia is a writer of YA fiction, a nature enthusiast and an avid photographer. She adores both cats and dogs. She is the editor and founder of online literary journal *Inside the Bell Jar,* which publishes fiction and poetry on mental illness. She also writes for online magazines *Bust* and *The Mighty*. As a sufferer of OCD, MDD and BPD, Autumn is currently housebound due to the severity of her conditions. It is for this reason that she dedicates a lot of her time advocating and campaigning for better mental health awareness.

Chris Baier is a content creator, copywriter and social media experimenter from Brooklyn, NY. His life parenting a child with a mental health disorder has morphed from clueless to advocate. Today, Chris is an activist for the OCD community in many ways, including: Co-produced UNSTUCK: An OCD Kids Movie, a documentary about kids who are OCD experts; runs an OCD support group for Parents of Children with OCD in NYC; advisor and "OCD Guru" at Wisdo; Blogger on The Mighty; Member and speaker at the OCD Foundation.

Kari Ferguson is a mom, Mormon, writer, and mental health advocate currently living in Washington state with her family. She graduated from Brigham Young University and then received her Master's Degree in Sociology, Communication, Culture and Society from Goldsmiths College, University of London. Kari served a mission for the Church of Jesus Christ of Latter-day Saints in northern Virginia before getting married and having two children. She documents her challenges and successes with having obsessive compulsive disorder while being LDS at theocdmormon.com.

ABOUT THE CURATOR

 Joshua Rivedal is the creator and founder of Changing Minds: A Mental Health Based Curriculum and **The i'Mpossible Project**. He is trained in human capital management with an emphasis in coaching from NYU, and is also trained in QPR, ASIST, and the teacher's edition of emotional intelligence at Yale University's Center for Emotional Intelligence. He has spoken about suicide prevention, mental health, diversity, and storytelling across the U.S., Canada, the U.K., and Australia. He currently serves on the advisory board of Docz, a startup peer-to-peer mental health app. He wrote and developed the one-man play, *Kicking My Blue Genes in The Butt* (KMBB), which has toured extensively throughout the world. His memoir *The Gospel According to Josh: A 28-Year Gentile Bar Mitzvah*, based on KMBB, is on The American Foundation for Suicide Prevention's recommended reading list. His second book, The i'Mpossible Project: Volume 1—*Reengaging with Life, Creating a New You*, debuted #1 in its category on Amazon in January 2016. He advises business owners on growth management, business building strategies, and marketing. He lives in Los Angeles with his wife, children, a cat, a hamster, two bunnies, and a guinea pig named Harriet.

ALSO BY JOSHUA RIVEDAL

The Gospel According to Josh:
A 28-Year Gentile Bar Mitzvah
(Based on the one-man show
Kicking My Blue Genes in the Butt)

By the time Joshua Rivedal turned twenty-five, he thought he'd have the perfect life—a few years singing on Broadway, followed by a starring role in his own television show. After which, his getaway home in the Hamptons would be featured in Better Homes & Gardens, and his face would grace the cover of the National Enquirer as Bigfoot's not-so-secret lover.

Instead, his resume is filled with an assortment of minor league theatre and an appearance on The Maury Povich Show—a career sidetracked by his father's suicide, a lawsuit from his mother over his inheritance, and a break-up with his long-term girlfriend.

Tortured by his thoughts, he finds himself on the ledge of a fourth-floor window, contemplating jumping out to inherit his familial legacy. In turn he must reach out to the only person who can help before it's too late.

Available on Amazon, Kindle, B&N.com. and at
www.iampossibleproject.com/the-gospel-according-to-josh

The i'Mpossible Project: Volume I
Reengaging with Life, Creating a New You

Storytelling is one of our oldest traditions. Stories can make us laugh or cry... or both at the same time. They can teach, inspire and even ignite an entire movement.

The i'Mpossible Project is a collection of powerful stories. They're gritty, deep, heartwarming... and guaranteed to help you discover new possibilities in your life.

These stories are all about overcoming obstacles, reengaging with life, and creating new possibilities—a son's homicide, a transgender man finding love, coming back from the brink of suicide, finding your funny in the face of overwhelming odds, and more...

If you're ready to create new possibilities in your life, you need to read this book!

Available on Amazon, Kindle, B&N.com. and at
www.iampossibleproject.com/one

A Mental Health Based Curriculum

Changing Minds is an evidence based curriculum that combines lecture, storytelling, group discussion, and improv theatre to enhance emotional development—providing hope, help, and lifesaving skills. Changing Minds is available for grades K-12, college, CEUs, and professional development.

There are five (5), sixty (60) minute modules:

- The Basics of Mental Health
- Developing Coping Skills
- Storytelling and Support Systems
- Living with/Supporting a Person with a Mental Health Condition
- Helping Yourself or a Friend in Suicidal Crisis

Five more modules are being developed on: Diversity, Emotional Intelligence, Anti-Bullying, and Substance Abuse.

www.iampossibleproject.com/changing-minds

CPSIA information can be obtained
at www.ICGtesting.com
Printed in the USA
LVOW13s0353100817
544407LV00040B/2340/P